THE IRREGULAR VERSES OF RUPERT BROOKE

British Library Cataloguing-in-publication data
A catalogue record for this book is available from the
British Library.
ISBN 0 9526031 3 6

First published in 1997 by Green Branch Press,
Kencot Lodge, Kencot, Lechlade, Gloucestershire GL7 3QX,
United Kingdom.
Tel. 01367 860588. Fax 01367 860619.

Typeset by Green Branch Press.

Printed and bound by Severnside Printers Limited,
Bridge House, Upton-upon-Severn, Worcestershire
WR8 0HG

The

IRREGULAR VERSES

of

RUPERT BROOKE

arranged with commentary

by

PETER MILLER

Green Branch

This work is
most affectionately dedicated
to my wife:
she has had to live with it,
bear with it
and read it:
all three things she has done
admirably

Some say thy fault is youth, some wantonness,
Some say thy grace is youth and gently sport;
Shakespeare, *Sonnet LXXXXVI*

Frère, voila pourquoi les poètes, souvent,
Buttent à chaque pas sur les chemins du monde.
Théophile Gautier, *Terza Rima*

Contents

ACKNOWLEDGEMENTS

For the help they have given I am indebted to the following:

Archives of Rugby School, and in particular the Archivist, Rusty MacLean, for provision of original material from *The Phoenix* and permission to reproduce its cover;

Faber & Faber, for permission to include quotations from the *Letters of Rupert Brooke* ed. Keynes, and Hassall's *Rupert Brooke: a Biography*

Pippa Harris for permitting the use of material from *Song of Love*;

The late Hugh Phillips for a careful reading and appraisal of my text;

The Provost and Fellows of King's College, Cambridge, and particularly Jacqueline Cox, the Modern Archivist of King's College, for a photocopy of *Choir Practice;*

Mike Read for supplying material from Brooke's copy of 'Horace' and encouragement to publish same.

Gareth and Anne Redd for supplying original latin texts and translations, and for invaluable help in interpretation.

The Trustees of the Rupert Brooke Estate for permission to reproduce copyright items which do not appear in either the *Letters of Rupert Brooke* ed. Keynes, or in Hassall's *Rupert Brooke: a Biography;*

And lastly I must name those, influential in their respective spheres, who have given me so much encouragement: Linda Hart, Patrick Quinn, Mike Read, Jon Stallworthy and Seán Street.

The portraits of Rupert Brooke are reproduced by courtesy of the National Portrait Gallery, London.

INTRODUCTION

'In writing an introduction such as this it is good to be brief.' So wrote Siegfried Sassoon in his 1920 introduction to the *Poems* of Wilfred Owen. A good injunction and one which I intend to follow here.

Sassoon knew Rupert Brooke quite well and wrote of an '. . . assured perception that I was in the presence of one on whom had been conferred all the invisible attributes of a poet.' (Hassall, p.451) He continued, 'Here, I might well have thought – had my divinations been expressible – was a being singled out for some transplendent performance, some enshrined achievement.' Virginia Woolf (p.529) thought much the same, though strangely, not as a poet – more as a politician she thought. Brooke had no illusions, however, and knew he might be thought of as only a minor poet, although he had contempt for such a classification, having said that one might as well speak of 'minor roses or minor sunsets' (p.92).

Rupert Brooke perhaps died too young to have achieved the 'transplendence' envisaged by Sassoon, but he was by instinct a poet and had been since childhood almost, so much so that he broke naturally into verse, as one might break into song. His letters are interspersed with doggerel rhymes, parodies, limericks and snatches of verse, and although some of his real, published, poetry does come near to achieving the level foreseen by Sassoon, it is this 'irregular' verse, compiled solely to amuse himself and others, which has such an endearing and entertaining quality.

The urge to versify bubbled up inside him; it started by flippant contributions to the alternative school magazine, *The Phoenix*, which he founded in 1904, and it ended just two weeks before his death, with comic verse about the discomforts of dysentery.

This collection is both for those who already know Brooke as well as for those who scarcely do. For those who do, light is shed on his character from different angles – not new perhaps but slanting diversely - and for those who don't a fascinating character is displayed. The various aspects of this character are implicit in the verses and the circumstances in which they were written, and I have tried in my commentaries to portray Brooke as he was – mercurial, often self-harming and diffident, sometimes perverse, hard and intolerant, but always enchanting to those who knew him.

I would like to think that this might be a bedside book – that readers, already pleasantly drowsy, might flick through the pages and be lulled off to sleep by this light-hearted essence of the Rupert Brooke who so liked to amuse his friends, and who was fully aware that one day his letters might be published. His friends seem to have obliged him by keeping them, and the task of publishing was meticulously executed by his lifelong friend and bibliographer Geoffrey Keynes in 1968. His *The Letters of Rupert Brooke*, together with Christopher Hassall's *Biography* (1964) are the principal sources of my present writing.

Nearly all these occasional verses have been, in their entirety, widely published before, except for the first four, three of which are drawn from old copies of *The Phoenix*. From *From a New Boy, To a Cadet Officer* and *Choir Practice* Hassall has published one stanza only. *A Form-Lesson*, I 'discovered' in a copy of *The Phoenix* in the Rugby School library, while the MS of *Choir Practice* is in the Brooke Archive at King's College, Cambridge.

When Rupert Brooke once told Keynes that he had given up writing, you can be sure he didn't mean it; his pen was never still and it is remarkable how much he wrote, both formal and informal, in the course of so short a life. I hope that his informal writings, collected together, will prove to be as entertaining as was the man himself, and that the commentaries will be biographically enlightening. I just felt that so much delight needed to be served up as a whole and garnished by a few remarks.

Peter Miller

From a New Boy

Hassall tells us that Rupert Brooke and another boy – the one who beat him in *The Pyramids* poetry competition – had been allowed to edit a supplement to the Rugby School magazine which they called *The Phoenix*. In its second issue appears a section contributed by Brooke called *A Child's Guide to Rugby School*. Under this heading, along with sundry comments of humorous irreverence about the school, there appears this verse entitled *From a New Boy*.

Punch printed one stanza in 1987, the centenary of Brooke's birth, with the comment that it showed he was a 'wimp' – that ubiquitous American cliché! Chambers Dictionary (1993) defines it as meaning 'a pusillanimous person'; that, Rupert Brooke certainly was not. He was not of course a new boy when he wrote it but was seventeen.

By the time he was sixteen he was playing cricket for his house and eventually played for the school in the First XI. When he was eighteen he became Head of House and was in the First XV. He is thus described in the school magazine: 'R. C. Brooke weighs 11 stone 12 lbs., and is a reliable centre three-quarter who, though not brilliant, is usually in his place, and makes good openings, he tackles too high.' (Hassall, p.77)

Why *Punch* chose to designate him a 'wimp' is to me a mystery – maybe it was just lack of research!

A framed transcription of the verse in which he described the scrum is to be found in the James Gilbert Rugby Football Museum, at Rugby. It seems a pretty good description of the feelings of a small boy quite new to the game, and the whole poem insists that Rugby's famous game is definitely not for him.

FROM A NEW BOY

Anonymously I indite
    These rhymes, dear Mr. Editor,
Since fellows are *so* impolite
    And I don't want my head hit, or
My person kicked with skill and force
    By those who think it right to root a
Defenceless New Boy, just because
    He does not like your nasty 'footer'.

And so I think that I'll remain
    Anonymous to all but you, Sir;
You, I am sure, will not disdain
    To hear my troubles, nor abuse a
Poor New Boy's trust; and – mark it well –
    My verses scan; *I* shan't insult your
Kind pages with such doggerel
    As shocks the readers of the *Vulture*

As you perceive, I'm rather young:
    I do not like the Rugby habits,
Nor this your strange barbarian tongue
    "To sweat, to groise, to oil, to cab," its
Most hard to learn. Although I try
    My best; and, further, may I put a
Plain question? – why on earth must I
Take part in low rough games of 'footer'?

When first I played I nearly died.
    The bitter memory still rankles –
They formed a scrum – with *me* inside!
    Some kick'd the ball, and some my ankles.
I did not like the game at all,
    Yet, after all the harm they'd done me,
Whenever I came near the ball
    They knocked me down, and stood upon me.

Cover of *The Phoenix*, March 1905   *Rugby School Archive*

They bade me collar as he paced
  One of great speed and massive figure;
I tried to seize him by the waist;
  He smote my nose – with painful vigour; –
      *   *   *   *

In short its one long gory fight; –
  Armenian massacres aren't in it, –
A carnage , whence the victim might
  Be snatched to Heaven any minute!

I never used to feel like this
  When I played Soccer, but at least I'm
Fully convinced that football is
  A fiendish and inhuman pastime.
Solemnly then I swear to you
  That henceforth – if you'll credit a
True tale – *The School Fifteen must do*
  WITHOUT ME, Mr. Editor.

1904

To a Cadet Officer

This verse was contributed anonymously to the third issue of *The Phoenix,* published in March 1905. In October, two months after his eighteenth birthday, Brooke became the Cadet Officer – a 2nd. Lieutenant – of the Rugby School Volunteer Rifle Corps. He had already attained the rank of colour-sergeant, so he must have, at least in part, taken his schoolboy military training with some degree of seriousness. This is borne out by the keenness with which he later trained at Blandford when a Sub-Lieutenant in the Royal Naval Division in 1914.

However, it was his habit to poke fun at and satirise almost everything that was part of the environment of his upbringing. This was a habit characteristic of Brooke throughout his short life; he was always ready to mock anything, including himself at times. Often though, he was ambivalent about those things he chose to satirise, and one must read between the lines when attempting to judge this side of his character. Those who knew him realised that his exuberant sense of fun overlaid much deeper – and indeed sometimes darker – sides of his mind.

In the Great War, Brooke's determination to fight the Germans had been reinforced by the horror he felt at having witnessed the sacking of Antwerp when serving with the Royal Naval Division. His cadet corps days a memory, their lightheartedness forgotten, Brooke was by then utterly resolved to lead his men and put his training to the test.

TO A CADET OFFICER

Ωφθη ξιφοσ εχων
['He was seen with a sword']
*cartoon caption from The Vulture magazine,
Rugby School, 24 June 1905.*

You asked me, "What's the Corps' most striking feature?
  As an outsider, tell me!" Well I knew
What I was meant to say, you funny creature, –
  I answered, 'You'.

Next, "What there was in *you* so very striking?"
  I've thought the question over, martial youth,
Here's my reply: (it mayn't be to your liking,
  But – it's the truth.)

'Tis naught wherewith the mere civilians taunt you,
  Tis not your frown, more mocked, alas! than feared, –
Not even your ghastly hat; (though that, I grant you,
  Is more than weird).

It's not that sword – unfailing block of stumbling –
  Not the remarks of cheeky errand boys;
It's none of these that sets the sections grumbling;
  It is – your voice.

1905

Choir Practice

This verse appears in a commonplace book that Rupert Brooke kept during his final year at Rugby. At this time he was struggling with his prize-winning poem *The Bastille*, neglecting his school work and trying to please his older literary friend, St. John Lucas, by producing poems to order. It tells us nothing about his attitude to music, but everything about his fondness for poking fun. In a public school of that era the school choir would have been fair game for mockery anyway.

For music he showed no particular aptitude while at school, though one of his best friends, Denis Browne, was a musician of remarkable talent. Because of this friendship he may have shown some interest in music while still at school, but he certainly did in later life, and while living at Grantchester he used frequently to go to concerts and the ballet in London.

Writing to Katharine Cox in 1911, he commented on feelings aroused by listening to Bach and Beethoven.

Also in 1911 he wrote to E.J.Dent:

> I thought it would be a nice occupation while I was working to take singing lessons. I don't want to sing much; and I don't imagine I should ever be able to. But I want to be able to get hold of airs; and chiefly I've an idea it might train my dreadfully uneducated ear a little. Which would be useful. (Keynes, Letters, p.317)

Did his 'uneducated ear' actually find the choir excruciating, or was it just his sense of fun – that sense of fun which has been commented upon by his schoolfriend Hugh Russell-Smith? I tend to think it was the latter.

CHOIR PRACTICE

O what is that weird wild wailing?
    Is it the song of a sorrowful cow?
Is't a bow-wow whose tail is down-trodden?
    Or pussy [remarking] miaow?

. . . .
    Of a bolt falling down from the sky.
. . . .
    When it catches one full in the eye.

O it rings through your ears like a brass band
    When it plays out of tune and, you know,
The fife's playing ten to the second
    And the kettledrum fifty or so.

The noise of a dog-fight is gentle,
    When compared to these heart-rending groans,
Which begin with a squeak in the treble,
    And descend very slowly to moans.

It plainly must be the choir practice,
    There is nothing but that which could make
Such a row, and then think it was music
    – Oh! stop it for harmony's sake!

1905

NOTE: The original MS of this poem is in the Brooke Archive at King's College, Cambridge: it had been, at one time, folded and heavily creased; thus some lines are obscured
by heavy dark markings and are, to all intents and purposes, illegible; lines 1 & 3, in
stanza 2, are such and cannot be reproduced. The 3rd. word in line 4, stanza 1, is also
partly illegible, and the word in brackets is here inserted on the grounds of probability,
and because it fits in with the, legible, beginning and end of the word.

A Form-Lesson
in triolets

Is this odd little poem biographical, or at least semi-biographical? It appeared in the last edition of *The Phoenix*, in March 1905. Throughout his scholastic and academic careers, Brooke, although possessed of a brilliant and original mind, was not noted for single-minded devotion to his studies.

Although he won the King's Medal for Prose, and the Poetry Prize with his poem *The Bastille*, and in his last term at Rugby gave a brilliant address to the school literary society, the headmaster reported on him finally as follows:

> His work is more uneven than any boy in the form; he either dislikes details or has no capacity for them. But when he is good – on the purely literary side of his work and scholarship he is capable of very brilliant results, and in English composition he must make a name. Always a delightful boy to work with. I am very sorry to lose him.

At Cambridge in 1907 Brooke wrote to a friend:

> I am in the middle of exams . . . I believe myself to be doing phenomenally badly. For the history (Greek . . . Roman) we had a year to prepare. I read 300 pages of Bury on the last two days and no Roman history at all. It quite reminded me of old times.

and to Hugh Russell-Smith a few weeks later:

> 'V' 'eard from me Tutor. Got a bad second in me Mays. Examiners held a special meeting 'to decide what steps to take in consequence of my "flippant remarks" in my History Papers'. (Keynes, Letters, p.88)

To Jacques Raverat he wrote in 1909 confessing that he had done no work for ages and that he was going to be a failure in his Tripos. In fact he got a rather poor second.

A FORM-LESSON
IN TRIOLETS

Just Before.

PUER   "It's my turn to go on?
　　　　　—And I don't know a word!
　　　　　You *might* give me a con,
　　　　　It's my turn to go on;
　　　　　—'Here he comes!' Then I'm done!
　　　　　—Oh, it's simply absurd;
　　　　　It's my turn to go on,
　　　　　And I don't know a word!"

During.

MAGISTER   "It's insufferable cheek –
　　　　　—*'You'd not got as far?'*
　　　　　You get lower each week! . . .
　　　　　—It's insufferable cheek . . .
　　　　　Write it—English and Greek.
　　　　　What a slacker you are!
　　　　　It's insufferable cheek,
　　　　　—'You'd not got as far!' "

Just After.

PUER   "He first jawed me: but then
　　　　　Bent me over a form . . .!
　　　　　I felt hopefuller, when
　　　　　He just jawed me. But *then* . . .
　　　　　—What? . . . About nine or ten!
　　　　　—Y-e-e-s; it *was* rather warm!
　　　　　He first jawed me; but then
　　　　　Bent me over a form!"

1905

21

The Slow Rain

In his preface to the *Poetical Works* Keynes writes, of Brooke's juvenilia, '. . . his early efforts acquire an interest for the evidence they afford of the influences at work during the formative years, even though their literary merit be not great.' (p.7)

This was Keynes's apology for including in his anthology earlier poems whose publication would probably not have been sanctioned by Brooke, had he lived. This poem was not included in the *Poetical Works* and its literary merit, with its strange use of italics and parentheses, and with its contrived mood and peculiar punctuation, is certainly not great. No doubt Brooke thought it was suitably 'Decadent' with its air of effete melancholy, a style he affected at the time, possibly under the influence of St John Lucas. (see also p.30)

Delany writes in *The Neo-Pagans*, '. . . he had been taken up by a local author, St John Lucas, a homosexual aesthete who was nine years older than Rupert.' (p.8) He adds, reassuringly, 'The relation seems to have been harmless enough.' Seeking to please Lucas, Rupert Brooke wrote in what he conceives to be the style, already becoming anachronistic, of *fin-de-siècle* poets such as Wilde and Dowson. In his last years at school he served up most of his poetry to Lucas for approval.

In a letter dated April 1905 he writes to Lucas, '. . . I *have* evolved twelve lines, which I enclose; but they are, I know, of a sort it is merely ridiculous for me to write.' (Keynes, Letters, p.24) He goes on to explain that the gloom was perhaps engendered by thoughts on *The Bastille*, a long poem he was working on, with which he eventually won the school's prize for poetry; at the time however he was despairing of any success, and said his mind was 'a Bastilian prosy paste.' (p.25)

Doubtless Brooke, ever self-critical, already realised what his friend Geoffrey Keynes later said – that the literary merit of his juvenilia was not great.

THE SLOW RAIN

Only the slow rain falling
　Sobs through the silence of this bitter place.
(And in my heart returns one pale lost face
　And the old voice calling, calling, . . .)

Only the grey dawn breaking
　Makes visible the long despair of rain.
(And from weariness of sleep I turn again
　To the weariness of waking, . . .

Only the dark wave crying
　Mocks ever the loneliness of hearts that yearn.
(Till from the weariness of Life at last I turn
　To the weariness of dying . . .)

1905

The Sea

In the summer of 1905 Rupert Brooke had chanced on a copy of the *Westminster Gazette*, in the Temple Reading Room at Rugby School, and found in it a poetry competition for the 'best Sicilian Otave . . .' He submitted an entry which was published in the July issue, although it did not win a prize. The next issue announced a competition for the best sonnet about the sea, which had to be written, as Hassall points out, to a rather elaborate specification.

The first eight lines had to describe the sea as a 'thronged ante-chamber', (Hassall, p.73) walled and roofed with emerald and silver and heaped with precious treasure. Then (the sestet) doors open at the blast of a trumpet . . . the 'pale company' shall enter with awe and wonder into the Presence, and rejoice . . . and they shall meet again those that mourned, but the chamber and treasure shall be left unheeded.

One is tempted to say, 'Phew!' – however, Brooke set to work on the principle 'All this has got to be got in somewhere', and using Wordsworth as his model in the octave and D.G.Rossetti in the sestet, he produced a prize-winning poem, *The Sea*. For this the *Westminster Gazette* paid him 10s. 6d. and printed it.

So *The Sea* was Rupert Brooke's first poem in public print and the money he received was his first ever literary fee. He subsequently won several more prizes from the same journal with nonsense verses or parodies occasioned by its successive competitions.

THE SEA

A hall of gleaming silence, ringed by sheer
  Unmoving emerald water; carpeted
With treasure-trove – pale pearls and coral red,
  And roofed with rippling silver. Far and near,
Vast crowds of late-awakened souls, who here
  Expect and wait – the sea's uncounted dead.
No sound, no stir, except when overhead
  The silver water wavers and grows clear.
Then hark, a trumpet call! The mighty throng
  Sways forward, finds the unencumbered place
Wherein all who have grieved and waited long
  Shall see at last their well-beloved's face.
Hushed is the homeless sea's unfinished song,
  Its treasures lie forgot in desert space.

1905

A Nursery Rhyme

This little poem was contributed to the Saturday problem page of the *Westminster Gazette* in a competition for the best new and original nursery rhyme. It did not win a prize, but did subsequently appear, with many pieces by other contributors, in the *Westminster Problems Book* published by Methuen & Co. in 1908.

This is described in a prefatory note to a small volume devoted to Brooke's juvenilia. It was edited by R.M.G. Potter and was published in a limited edition of 99 copies, at Hartford, Connecticut, in 1925. The editor's foreword to the book contains the following statement, which begins thus:

> That which is here presented is of the juvenilia of Rupert Brooke, with one exception. None of it has been included in any publishing of the poet's collected work hitherto. The verses from his copy of Horace, now in my possession, are here first printed.
>
> The book has been made for those who inseparably link and love the poet and his work. For them any illumination of this brilliant personality, however slight, will be of intense interest. For them the charm of these fragments will not be marred by their want of weight. (Keynes, *Bibliography* pp. 39-41)

A NURSERY RHYME

Up the road to Babylon,
  Down the road to Rome,
The King has gone a-riding out
  All the way from home.

There were all the folks singing,
  And the church-bells ringing,
When the King rode out to Babylon,
  Down the road to Rome.

Down the road from Babylon,
  Up the road from Rome,
The King came slowly back
  All the way back home.

There were all the folks weeping,
  And the church-bells sleeping,
When the King rode back from Babylon,
  When the King came home.

(say 1906)

Horace's Odes

The prefatory note from Potter's book (see page 26) makes mention of the three verses here printed. They were, it says, '. . . taken from Brooke's own copy of Horace used by him while at Rugby (School). Each is written in pencil on that page which bears the lines from which the translations were made.'

However they are hardly literal translations. Rather they are anachronistic paraphrases and witty parodies of Horace's latin, which cleverly imitate the form of his stanzas and to a certain extent his metre. The Persians ('Persicos' in Horace) were held by the Romans to be dissolute and effete, so Brooke's 'pomp of Paris' is probably a reference to the *fin-de-siècle* decadence of Paris, and is a deliberate anachronism, as is of course the pub waiter, etc.

Brooke's 'somewhat Gallic rhymes' may well refer to the French poet Baudelaire, whom he much admired. Horace simply refers to the muse of poetry.

Kipling is substituted for the epic Roman poet Varius, who wrote about military exploits, as did Kipling. The reference to Kipling and Homer and the lyre (and the banjo!) suggests that Brooke was probably familiar with Kipling's poem *When Omer Smote 'is Bloomin' Lyre* and also *The Song of the Banjo*.

Incidentally the former poem is a telling commentary on plagiarism, which, if it didn't influence Brooke, at least concurred with his own later commentary on the same subject in his dissertation *John Webster and the Elizabethan Drama*, in which he suggested that the Elizabethans had healthy and sensible views on the subject, 'They practised and encouraged the habit [of plagiarism]. Webster and his fellow-dramatists were all plagiarists', he said. (Brooke, Webster, pp146-7) Brooke defended plagiarism, but was himself more of an imitator than a plagiarist.

Brooke's verses on 'Horace, Liber 1, Carmen xxxvii' were also published by Timothy Rogers, in his Centenary Edition of Brooke's poems. Rogers however numbers Carmen 38, *correctly*: but Potter is in error also with 17, which should be 16.

HORACE'S ODES

Fellow, I hate your pomp of Paris,
Those neat green garlands you propose.
No longer seek the spot where tarries
The last red rose.

We only want some simple shrub
That will disgrace nor you, the stripling
Waiter, nor me in village pub
Placidly tippling.

Liber 1, Carmen xxxviii.

Kipling the bard, our latest scion of Homer,
Shall hymn thee on the lyre (or banjo) strings;
Thee, both on land and sea victorious roamer
And other things.

Liber I, Carmen vi.

A few small fields I have from fate,
A trick of somewhat Gallic rhymes,
And most unfeignedly to hate
These vulgar times.

Liber II, Carmen xvii.

(say 1906)

An Easter Day Song

St. John Welles Lucas was a minor poet, essayist and literary critic, some nine years older than Rupert Brooke. He lived in Rugby and is chiefly to be remembered for having edited *The Oxford Book of French Verse* (1907). He was responsible for interesting the young Brooke in the 'decadent' writers and poets of the preceding decade such as Wilde, Dowson, Swinburne, etc., also the French poet Baudelaire.

He encouraged the young man, whom he recognised as talented. As a result, for about three years, Brooke submitted most of his juvenilia to him for approval, and wrote to him poems and letters which were affectedly 'decadent' in style – a style that he fondly hoped would appeal to Lucas.

In May 1906 Brooke wrote a letter to Lucas which included a poem and its explanation, which reads as follows:

> The School musician[1], a youth of 18 who knows Arthur Eckersley[2] and composes fluently sent me a request that I should give him a song to set to music. The idea irritated me so much that I complied. With much labour I hammered out a 'song'. It is unlike other songs. It is called 'A Song in praise of Cremation, written to my lady on Easter Day'. It treats in, a laboured cunning metre, of the discomforts of being buried in a grave. It is closely modelled on Baudelaire's 'The Corpse'. How he received it I have not heard; but I think it will satisfy him. I am eager to hear the music. (Keynes, Letters, p.52)

Keynes notes in *The Letters of Rupert Brooke* that there are two versions of the Easter-Day Song, of which this, written in the hand of Denis Browne, seems to be the final one.

[1] W. Denis Browne was with Brooke, later, in the Royal Naval Division, formed one of his burial party, wrote about it in a series of letters, and was himself killed at Gallipoli. He was a brilliant musician.

[2] Arthur Eckersley also lived in Rugby: a dramatist and contributor to *Punch*.

AN EASTER DAY SONG

In Praise of Cremation written to my Lady Corsyra

Suddenly, at the pale death whisper, I
    Must go
Down to the cruel dark, and lie
Remembering thy lips, and know
Upon, around, within my helpless form
    The feeding worm.

I loathe the unseen darkness of the tomb;
    —To lie
Through the slow hours of stifling gloom
In shameful, helpless, agony,
Changed by the worms' unnatural cold lust
    To slime and dust!

Far in the lonely night, the rain and cold
    To sleep
Till through the gloomy, putrid mould
    The blind, lewd things that mouth and creep
Fondle and foully kiss these lips anew,
    Once kissed by you.

Rather for me the sudden flame's embrace
    Which clings
Once . . . , and therewith the perfect face
    Shall fade, the last of mortal things
So for all time I'll quench my hot desire
    In that clean fire.

1906

[1] The name is spelt 'Coesyra' in *The Letters*, but 'Corsyra' in *The Biography*: the first may be a misprint; the latter looks right and sounds better.

To my Lady Influenza

It was Geoffrey Keynes, Brooke's bibliographer and friend of both his Rugby and Cambridge days, who, when Brooke had joined him at university, tried to persuade him to give up his mannered and derivative decadent pose – or poses.

Brooke's initial defence of his affectations were expressed thus:

> I have thought over your idea of my at length giving up the pose of discontent and taking to optimism in my old age. I think not . . . And a week today I shall return to Cambridge! . . . And I shall be rather witty and rather clever & I shall spend my time pretending to admire what I think it humorous or impressive in me to admire. Even more than yourself I attempt to be 'all things to all men'; rather 'cultured' among the cultured, faintly athletic among athletes, a little blasphemous among blasphemers, slightly insincere to myself . . .

> However there are advantages in being a hypocrite aren't there? One becomes Godlike in this at least, that one laughs at all the other hypocrites. (Keynes, Letters, p.73)

As usual this is written flippantly, though there is an underlying motif of criticism of the pretentious – of hypocrites in fact! Shortly after this he did in fact begin to abandon his decadent pose – which wouldn't have gone down well at Cambridge anyway.

The Influenza sonnet which he wrote out at the end of the letter to Keynes, was, he said, - 'probably the work of Oscar Wilde, at least of his school.' This was one of his last Wildean affectations, clever, witty, full of 'decadent' ideas and really a parody.

TO MY LADY INFLUENZA

As rode along the paven ways of Rome
   Isis, and smiled imperturbably,
While monstrous eunuchs yapped in obscene glee;
   Or perhaps rather as thou us'd'st to come,
Phoibos, in all thy pale pink nudity;
   Or *she* (wearing a fillet on her brow
And absolutely naught else) from the sea
   Rising, an argent dawn! so cometh now
My Lady *Influenza*, like a star
   Inebriously wan, and in her train
Fever, the haggard soul's white nenuphar,
   And lily-fingered *Death*, and grisly *Pain*,
And *Constipation*, who makes all things vain,
   Pneumonyer, Cancer, and Nasal Catarrh.

1906

Ballade (To J.B.S[trachey].)

This was suggested by a pamphlet issued by some agency for promoting purity among the young by informing them of physiological facts, which angered Rupert Brooke. The fourth and eighth lines in each stanza are quotations from it. The Centenary Edition (1987) of Brooke's poems (edited by Timothy Rogers), is my only source of this poem, and the above sentence is a direct quotation from that work.

BALLADE (TO J.B.S[TRACHEY].)

Boys! mine is not a pleasant task to-day;
But to the pure everything is pure.
(Levinstein do not fidget!) Let us pray . . .
You often must have noticed, I am sure,
When washing in your little tub or ewer,
Or wondering How God fashioned you, or worse
Yielding to Curiosity's base lure, –
Between your legs there hangs a bag, or purse.

Sir! have you wondered why the world is grey?
Why I am grim and hollow-eyed, and you're
Snappy, and She is singing all the day?
(You often must have noticed, I am sure),
Some say, the higher that we go, the fewer,
Some, there's a purpose in the universe . . .
Look down, young man! The thing is not obscure
Between your legs there hangs a bag, or purse.

1906

A Scrabbly Epithet

Brooke had a great friend at Rugby School, Hugh Russell-Smith, to whom he often wrote, frequently in flippant vein.

One gets the impression that Brooke wrote letters full of comic nonsense, as much to amuse himself as well as his friends. These friends, no doubt, found these letters amusing – so many have been kept and published; they knew their friend, they could read between the lines and could dissect out which parts of the letter – or indeed which of his letters – were serious and which were nonsensical froth.

To Katharine Cox he confessed, '. . . I write driftingly and madly . . .' (Keynes, Letters, p.308) One can only agree: yes, he does, frequently – but of course his letters are very revealing, as well as being entertaining.

In the letter containing this poem, apart from using 'A fictitious word' (Keynes) in Greek characters, Δηρυ, which he urges on Russell-Smith as a kind of mantra, he tells him if he has cold baths and a *light* breakfast, and concentrates on the mystic word all day long he will become successful – he doesn't say in what.

He ends by saying

You know I always like to keep you *au fait* (as our Gallic neighbours would have it) with my latest literary activity. This came to me as I was sitting by the sea the other day. I don't know what it was – perhaps it was the rhythm of the waves. But I felt I must sing. So I sang: (Keynes, Letters, p.86)

A SCRABBLY EPITHET

I love a *scrabbly* epithet,
The sort you can't ever forget,
That blooms, a lonely violet
In the eleventh line of a sonnet.

I know one such; I'm proud to know him.
I'll put him in my next GREAT POIM.
He plays the psack-butt very well:
And his aunt was a Polysyllable.

1907

Lulworth

In July 1907 Brooke wrote to his friend Geoffrey Keynes, saying:

> But you shouldn't ask for a 'real letter' as of old. Aren't we a little too
> wise for the nonsense that once amused us? (Keynes, Letters, pp. 93-94)

He then wrote a page or two of what was more or less nonsense and enclosed further pages of lighthearted twaddle in the form of a newspaper, headed: **THE PIMPINELLA PALACE[1] POST**

This 'paper' carries such items as 'Special Interview', 'Notes on Dress', 'Poetical Corner' (including a few lines that might have come from William McGonagall):

> *Topographical Sonnet*
> Lulworth is one of the most delectable of towns,
>   Being pleasantly situated among downs
> Some of them hundreds of feet large, and more,
>   Such as I never saw
> Before.
> On the other side of it
> Are the billows of the ocean.

Then there is 'Interview with Gaffer Plugg' and 'Poiticle Adres, wrot by Me and Ugh, Hour Marx . . .X . . X'; at the end of all this tomfoolery come the verses about Lulworth.

In this letter he mentions that while clambering on rocks near the sea his copy of Keats's poems fell into the water and he had to go in after it. Years later he learned that these rocks had been the last place Keats had stood in England. From thence the dying poet had gone back aboard his ship and wrote his last poem and sailed for Italy.

[1]Brooke's name for his lodgings at Lulworth.

LULWORTH

Verse I
Oh give our love to Lulworth Cove,
And Lulworth Cliffs and Sea!
Oh Lulworth Down! Oh Lulworth Town!
(The name appeals to me.)
If we were with you today in Lulworth,
How happy we should be!
Verse II
The Lulworth downs are large and high
And honourable things.
There we would lie (old Hugh and I!)
On the tombs of the old sad kings:
If you lie up there, with your face in the grass
You can hear their whisperings.
Verse III
And each will sigh for the good day light
And for all his ancient bliss.
Red wine, and the fight, and the song by night,
Are the things they chiefly miss.
And one, I know, (for he told me so)
Is sick for a dead lad's kiss.
Verse IV
Ah! they're fain to be back for a many things
But mainly (they whisper) these:
England and April (the poor dead kings!)
And the purple touch on the trees,
And the women of England, and English springs
And the scent of English seas.
Verse V
But a lad like you, what has he to do
With the Dead, be they living or dead,
And their whims and tears for what can't be theirs?
Live you in their silly stead,
With a smile and a song for the live and strong
And a sigh for the poor old Dead.

Verses VI to LX
Still simmering

1907

Memling

Rupert Brooke had a friend who formed part of his Cambridge circle. He was in his early forties during Rupert's undergraduate years and worked at the University Library. His name was Charles Sayle and he lived in Trumpington Street and kept open house to many students.

Brooke wrote to him from Belgium. (Keynes, Letters, pp. 108) He was on a tour with his family and had left them to spend a few days in Antwerp with his brother, sightseeing and looking at art treasures. He said he loved especially some of the Vandycks and Franz Hals's pictures but emphatically not others of the earlier schools.

Elsewhere he said that he didn't like the early Dutch masters for being too lifelike – which reality he finds depressing. This particular letter ends with a rhyme about it.

Brooke was intensely interested in all forms of visual art, and soon was to earn himself a reputation of being a sound gallery critic, contributing articles on art exhibitions to national journals and newspapers.

As so often with Brooke, this rhyme is best judged for its entertainment value rather than its sincerity.

MEMLING

From too much love of Memling,
From John van Eyck set free,
I swear, without dissembling,
They don't appeal to me.
Rubens is far too clever
Vandyck & Teniers never
Could captivate
Yours ever
Profoundly
R.C.B.

[Exigencies of metre & rhyme dictate the frigid haughtiness of the close. RUPERT]

1907

A Fabian?

Rupert Brooke was involved with politics from boyhood. His mother was a lifetime worker for, and leader of, the Liberal cause in Rugby, and in the general election of 1906 the entire Brooke family was enlisted in the Liberal cause. Rupert, recovering from a fever, rose from his bed and went canvassing for Corrie Grant, the Liberal candidate and subsequently Rugby's MP, while Parker Brooke, Rupert's father, had accompanied Grant to make his deposition. Rupert's brothers also went canvassing.

At Cambridge, however, Brooke soon moved further to the left and under the influence of the Webbs and Bernard Shaw and others, he joined the Cambridge Fabian Society in 1907. In 1908 he signed the 'Basis', which was essentially a declaration of assent and agreement with the Fabian aims, and a prerequisite of full membership. He subsequently became its President.

In a letter to Geoffrey Keynes, dated January 1909, he makes a reference to Blake (Keynes, in later life, became a leading authority on Blake) and also to the Fabians in two obscurely comic and untitled quatrains.

He assures Keynes that he has given up writing, and in another letter, written at about the same time, to someone else, he says, 'I do not work or write. I read Socialist books for me country's good. Ha! Ha!' We can take this with a pinch of salt – he was always writing something. He says that he tried to do Keynes a sonnet about things he would understand . . . but that it wasn't much good. The resulting quatrains were 'in' jokes which Keynes probably enjoyed. At any rate he prints them in *The Letters*. (Keynes, Letters, p.155)

A FABIAN?

One began something like this –

Poor dear Mr Punnett[1]
Has gone and done it
They say he's a Fabian
Or very likely *may* be one. . .

And there was another, about –

Prof. Weissman[2]
Can *hardly* be a nice man,
If he thinks that to be a Blakian mystic
Is merely a recessive Mendelian characteristic.

1909

[1] R.C.Punnett, afterwards Professor of Genetics at Cambridge
[2] August Weissman, (1834-1914), Professor of Zoology, Freiburg im Breisgau, 1866-1914, studied evolution: his theories of heredity, that acquired characteristics are not directly transmitted, were contrary to Lamarckian theory and are now generally accepted.

To Two Old School Friends

In September 1909, in the course of a long letter to Dudley Ward, Rupert Brooke says, '. . . yesterday the Westminster [*Gazette*] promised me two guineas for half an hour's despicable work.' (Keynes, Letters, p.183)

Hassall, in *The Biography*, states that Brooke's nonsense verse or parodies, occasioned by the *Westminster Gazette* competitions, had proved consistently successful and had won him several prizes. *To Two Old School Friends* was one of the titles suggested and the entry had to be accompanied by the writer's own critical commentary.

Hassall goes on to suggest that Brooke's entry may have something to do with the impact of his first meeting with Justin Brooke, in whose eyes Rupert 'had seemed so excessively urban'. Brooke, of Emmanuel College, was no relation to Rupert, but was in fact the son of the founder of the Brooke Bond tea business. Brought up on his father's country estate, he was very much a countryman. They became friends when Rupert was persuaded to play the part of the Herald in the *Eumenides* of Aeschylus which was being produced by the Greek Play Committee; later they joined the Marlowe Society when it was founded in 1907.

In the commentary that accompanies his poem, Brooke writes:

There is Poetry. The *images* are clear and fascinating; the turns of *phrase* individual; the i*dea* not blatantly obvious, but subtly important; the *metre* boldly licentious and utterly successful . . . What *verve*! I have not faltered in my wonder and admiration of this poem for weeks, not since May 9, the day I wrote it. (Hassall, p.200)

TO TWO OLD SCHOOL FRIENDS

What! make you mouths, O twain mad dreamers, yet,
   You of the woodland, of the city you?
   Still mock you at me as 'between the two',
As 'torpid, dull, suburban'? You forget;
The soul is its own place. And mine is rife,
   Even mine, in spite of all that mother says,
   With wine, and song, red night and sunless days,
And life! Life amorous! Even in Balham, life!
Know you of Nature? . . . Down our street there grow
Trees, iron-fenced! whose names I do not know.
Of Art? . . . My wall-paper is greenish grey,
   And all my ties of a sad umber shade.
Of Life? . . . Upon the landing, yesterday,
   I suddenly kissed the under-parlourmaid.

1909

The Shepherd Doran His Dumpe

Another *Westminster Gazette* competition required that a poem be written in the manner of some minor poet of a past age. Brooke's entry was in imitation of Robert Greene, and he deservedly won first prize for it.

Greene (1558-92), who died supposedly of a surfeit of hock and herrings, but more probably of the plague, was '. . . a feckless drunkard, who abandoned his wife and children to throw himself on the mercies of tavern hostesses and courtesans,' according to the *Oxford Companion to English Literature*. He nevertheless wrote some charming and appealing songs and lyrical poems.

Like Brooke he had many detractors, but his principal apologist said of him, 'Hee inherited more vertues than vices.' This too we can happily say about Brooke!

This clever parody is a satirical sequel to *Doron's Description of Samela*. Ironically the fifth line in Brooke's second stanza proves to be prophetic. A little more than three months after Ka had given herself to the importunate yearning Rupert, early in February, following their rendezvous at Verona, he wrote to Jacques Raverat (24 May 1912): 'I go about with the woman, dutifully . . .Love her? – bless you, no: but I don't love anybody. The bother is I don't really *like* her, at all . . .' His relationship with Ka remained unresolved to the end of his life.

THE SHEPHERD DORAN HIS DUMPE

A Pritty Lamentable Ditty of Love's Flighte
(attributed to Ro. Greene)

Mine Harte, that like to Salamanders burn'd
   Is now growne Colde;
Mine eyes, that wept for Love Unkinde, are turn'd
   Even to Stones, that have no Lust for Seeing;
Cupid, that in my Brest to Dwel was bolde,
   Is Fled, and my Sadde Songs pursue him Fleeing;
Ah Love: swete Love, whose prettie Torments erst did
shake me,
False Love, ah Love, alas! if thou wilt now
Forsake me!

Saméla, her that was mine Onely Deere,
   I seek no more;
Nor doth her Beautie move mee, tho' so Cleare
   It shines, not Venus' Selfe I holde Above her.
I love her Not , who Loved soe wel before,
   and what's her Beautie, sith I cannot Love her?
Ah Love swete Love, whose prettie Torments erst did
shake me,
False Love, ah Love, alas! if thou wilt now
Forsake me!

Thus I, long time that Groned in Cupid's Thrall,
   May now Goe Free
Yet of my Freedome take no Ioie at all.
   My Praier being Granted turnes to mine Undoing,
And that I love not More Tormenteth mee
   Than ever Love didde, or my Vain pursueing:
Ah Love: swete Love, whose prettie Torments erst did
shake me,
False Love, ah Love, alas! if thou wilt now
Forsake me!

1909

A Limerick

Hugh Russell-Smith was a great friend of Rupert Brooke's, at school, and after they had both taken up classical scholarships at King's College Cambridge.

Brooke used to stay with the Russell-Smith family at Watersgreen House, Brockenhurst. Hassall tells of his happiness there in the midst of a young family of brothers and sisters and that ' . . . he was in no hurry to rejoin his own family circle that seldom made light of things and was given to such long silences at meals.'

After Brooke's death Russell-Smith, who was himself later killed in action wrote, in the school magazine, *The Meteor:*

'For the first two or three years, I think, few of us realised that someone out of the ordinary had come among us. He was rather shy and quiet though he at once proved himself a good athlete, . . . he used to go off to read the reviews of books in the *Morning Post* and *Chronicle*. He read Walter Pater and authors we knew very little about. He read a good deal of poetry, . . . But it was his personal charm that attracted us most, his very simple and lovable nature . . . (Marsh, p.9)

This limerick is the main feature of a postcard which he wrote to his friend Hugh from Clevedon, dated 21 August 1909. He asks whether Hugh will be at Brockenhurst after Sept. 6th, adding 'I fear not'; he also adds, 'I don't like my family'.

In a 'testamentary' letter written five weeks before Brooke's death and marked 'If I die to be sent to Dudley Ward' (one of his closest friends) he mentions Russell-Smith as one of the friends who 'might want books or something of mine'. (Hassall, p.518)

A LIMERICK

This is to remind you I have got yr Bradley
(Lectures on Shakespearian Tragedy)
    I read it very readily
    For he writes not at all badly
Though he has the usual Oxford malady[1]

1909

[1] Muzzy Mind

Railway Lines

Hugh Dalton, in later life Chancellor of the Exchequer in Attlee's government, was one of Brooke's undergraduate friends and a fellow-member of the Cambridge Fabian Society. Brooke frequently wrote to him.

Brooke and Dalton were colleagues in socialism and indeed it was from Dalton that he first sought guidance in joining the Fabians. It was at the end of his term as President of the Fabians at Cambridge that Brooke delivered his address *Democracy and the Arts*[1]. The Arts Council was formed in 1946 when Dalton was Chancellor of the Exchequer. One feels that had Brooke lived he would have played a very considerable part in its foundation.

By 1909, according to Hassall, Brooke was ending his involvement in Fabian affairs and was even then gently poking fun at the philosophy of G.E.Moore[2] which had influenced so many undergraduate minds of Brooke's generation. Moore, at one time described by Brooke as 'the greatest living philosopher', taught that 'good states of mind' were necessary. Apparently 'good', though highly subjective and indefinable, described a state of mind essential to the proper conduct of aesthetic and emotional life, and of the life of the senses. Reason had to guide feeling, and logic, the state of mind.

It was inevitable that Brooke, although influenced by this teaching, should choose to make fun of it. Hence this rhyme in a letter to Dalton. (Keynes, Letters p.169) Perhaps at the age of twenty-two its influence was beginning to wane, as was already the influence of Fabianism.

---

[1] *Democracy and the Arts (a hitherto unpublished essay) by Rupert Brooke,* preface by G.L.Keynes, Rupert Hart Davis, London, 1946

[2] *Principia Ethica*, by G.E.Moore

RAILWAY LINES

['I have made a *very* good Anti-Nature Poem to Railway
Lines on Which I Suddenly Came When Walking on
the Edge of Dartmoor; Being Tired of Irregular Things.
It begins . . . ']

'O straight and true! straight and true! . . . '

['and further on there's a verse']

'For no laws there be in Sky and Sea,
  And no Will in the wayward Wood;
Nor no States of Mind in the Gypsy Wind,
  – The which alone are good.'

['it halts a little, perhaps.']   R.

1909

Justin's Beard

Justin Brooke, already mentioned in this work (p.44), had left university in 1908, but in 1910 was still involved with the Cambridge Marlowe Society. While the society was engaged in putting on a repeat performance of Marlowe's *Doctor Faustus* for a party of fifty German students, they were eagerly awaiting Justin's return from a long absence in Canada. Frances Cornford[1] was, in his absence, handling all the casting problems, including finding suitable people to play the Seven Deadly Sins. So great were these difficulties that Rupert wrote to say that he had discovered an Eighth Deadly Sin – the Artistic Temperament.

Justin eventually returned from Canada displaying a (presumably totally unexpected) recently grown beard.

Rupert had accepted a minor part in *Doctor Faustus* – a brief appearance as the Chorus in a scholar's gown and black skull-cap, but he was busy with Fabian affairs that summer, and his liaison with the project, until Justin's return, was with Mrs. Cornford. He wrote from Rugby, where he was staying at his mother's home at 24 Bilton Road.

At that time he was making arrangements to tour Southern England in a caravan with his friends Dudley Ward and Keeling,[2] in order to publicise the Minority Report of the Poor Law Commission. Rumour had reached him that Justin had returned bearded from the Western World; so, in a letter to his friend Jacques Raverat he seeks confirmation of the rumour in the form of a limerick.

---

[1] wife of Francis Cornford, a junior classics don at Trinity College, Cambridge

[2] Dudley Ward & F. (Ben) Keeling, Brooke's undergraduate contemporaries: Keeling was killed on the Somme.

JUSTIN'S BEARD

Is it true that our Justin's appeared?
Has he come, as we all of us feared,
  Not the Justin we knew,
  But Western, but new,
With an Accent, a Soul, and a BEARD?

1910

Easter, and the End-of-Term (1.)

On January 24th 1910 William Parker Brooke, Rupert's father, died of a stroke, aged 59. His funeral took place on the very day his boys returned to School Field for the Easter Term, and Rupert, who had been helping his mother through the difficult period of his father's decline, became acting housemaster for the remainder of the term. He caught 'flu at the funeral and started his term by being in bed; he relates that he was ill and ' . . . subsisted on milk and the pieces I could surreptitiously bite out of my thermometer'.

By his own account he was quite a success as a housemaster. As he wrote to Edward Marsh, 'Being a Housemaster is in a way pleasant. The boys are delightful; & I find I'm an admirable schoolmaster'. (Keynes, Letters, p.224)   At the end of term he wrote a long, impromptu verse letter, in rhyming couplets, to his friend Dudley Ward, who was by then a correspondent for the *Economist* in Germany. (p.230)

This letter is written from his new address.   In arranging his housemastership, Brooke and his mother had secured to their own advantage an extra term of income and breathing space to look around for somewhere to live. The move, when it came, was to a not very attractive rented house, and Brooke undoubtedly found the move a wrench. He had loved the garden and tennis court at School Field. Poignantly Hassall tells us, 'Tibby the cat, aged sixteen, was given the quietus of poison in her milk.' (Hassall, p.219)

To Marsh he wrote:

'For the rest of Eternity my stabile address is 24 Bilton Road, Rugby. School Field, that palatial building, will know us no more. And henceforth I shall have to play on other people's Tennis lawns. I wept copiously last week in saying goodbye to the three-and-fifty little boys whose Faith & Morals I had upheld for ten weeks. I found I had fallen in love with them all. So pleasant & fresh-minded as they were.' (Keynes, Letters, p.234)

EASTER, AND THE END-OF-TERM (1)

To Dudley Ward
(24 Bilton Road for the future)
[27 March 1910]

Easter! the season when One had rebirth
Whom some call Ishtar, some call Mother Earth,
And others Jesus, or Osiris. Now
A certain subtle magic on the bough
And a bright strangeness in the wind (a sort
Not known in Germany or here) has brought,
These hundred centuries past, the bloody rotters
Who lusted, raped, and (knowing not) begot us
– In fact, our fathers, from remotest times –
To sing in company, make foolish rhymes,
Lust more than ever, dance, drink wine, eat bread,
To greet the jolly spring. And they are Dead.
(And lately – since the Greeks – they've spoilt the feast
With morbid superstitions from the East.
E'en now small boys at chapel down the road
Munch little morsels of a Jewish God.)
Easter, you bloody man! And a full moon!
And so I think of you; and write . . .

Brooke's rhyming letter to Ward, dated 27 March 1910, is too long to print here in its entirety, but as printed in the *Letters* it is certainly worth reading right through for the sake of amusement. The first part bears little relationship to its last part, and the two portions are here given separately. The first shows Brooke as the *agnogger*[1] he frequently claimed to be.

From that time on Bilton Road played a very considerable part in Brooke's life. Many of his letters are written from this address. Although in his younger years he could not endure to spend too long in his mother's presence, he constantly returned to her and spent a good deal of time working and writing in Rugby. When he came home from America in 1913, he looked forward eagerly to reunion with his mother, the very real fondness he had for her having been reinforced by absence.

It was at Bilton Road that Brooke on Christmas leave from the Navy, in 1914, prepared for publication his five war sonnets. They had been written at Blandford camp, while he was under training as a Sub-Lieutenant in the Royal Naval Division. He had sent a set of proofs to Cathleen Nesbitt; in her auto-biography she quotes from the accompanying letter:

'My muse panting all autumn under halberd and cuirass could but falter these syllables through her visor. God they are in the rough these five camp children. Four and five are good though and there are phrases in the rest. Forgive me if I include ours[2] among them . . . Only we will know, and it seems to belong with them.' (Nesbitt, p.95)

He left his mother and 24 Bilton Road, for London, on New Years Day 1915. She never saw him again.

---

[1] Brooke's word for *agnostic*

[2] *Sonnet II, Safety*

EASTER, AND THE END OF TERM (2)

For now – the days ebb to a close: and I
Shall soon be no more pedagogue. I fly
On Wednesday hence to London – *Justice!* . . .
I meet my freedom quietly. I get
A certain pleasure from the fifty dam
Young fresh-faced mindless scamps to whom I am
Father, and mother, and all their maiden aunts.
I feed their minds. I satisfy their wants.
I train them, cane them, lie to them (for truth
Is not revealed to impressionable youth).
They are upper-class. They do not know the Light.
They stink. They are no good. And yet . . . in spite
Of the thousand devils that freeze their narrowing views
(Christ, and gentility, and self-abuse)
They are young, direct, and animal. In their eyes
Spite of the dirt, stodge, wrappings, flits and flies
A certain dim nobility. They are MAN,
Still, for a year or two . . . And so they can
– In mind *and* body – not unawkwardly move,
At times . . . in the sun . . . in April . . .
                              So I love
(Partly because to live it, once, I found
All glory, and . . . there are . . . spots of holy ground
– Oh, mildly holy! – about the place!) each line
Of the fine limbs and faces; love, in fine,
(O unisexualist!) with half a heart,
Some fifty boys, together, and apart,
Half-serious and half-sentimentally . . .
– But, by the 6th, all this thing ends for me . . .

1910

A Letter to a Shropshire Lad

The poet A.E.Housman was made Professor of Latin at Cambridge in 1911, at the age of 52. At that time Rupert Brooke was living in Munich, where he had gone to learn German. Every morning he used to go to a certain café to read *The Times* and thus it was that he first learned of Housman's appointment.

That same week Brooke had won a competition in *The Saturday Westminster*. It was for 'the best new and original letters to live poets'. Brooke's *Letter to a Live Poet*, which won the prize, began, 'Sir, since the last Elizabethan died . . . ' This was eventually published in the *Collected Poems*, 1918. However at the same time he had submitted another entry. Keynes notes, in *The Letters*, that the prizewinning entry was printed in *The Saturday Westminster* for 4 February 1911, and that the alternative entry, *Letter to a Shropshire Lad*, was printed in the issue of 13 May.

Brooke's 'other idea', as Hassall calls it, was subtitled, 'apropos, more or less of a recent appointment' and it was a gently witty parody, suggesting that as Housman had been appointed to teach Latin he should give up writing poetry. A clever take-off of the rhyme and metre of Housman's distinctive ballad form, it is immediately recognisable as an imitation of the famous *A Shropshire Lad*, and here and there takes and twists lines which are obviously identifiable.

The first stanza, for example, is a direct skit on Housman's verse – No. 50 begins thus:

> Clunton and Clunbury,
> Clungford and Clun,
> Are the quietest places
> Under the sun . . . .

. . . and it is this poem too whose last verse is imitated by Brooke's last verse, while Housman's 'And little 'twill matter to one' becomes, in Brooke's poem, 'And it's little one will care.' Housman's No.44 is imitated in the second verse and, further on, 'Undishonoured, clear of 'danger' becomes 'Undishonoured, clean and clear.' 'Oh lad, you died as fits a man' (No.19) becomes 'Oh, lad, you chose the better way'. 'And the name died before the

A LETTER TO A SHROPSHIRE LAD

(Apropos, more or less, of a recent appointment)

Emmanuel, and Magdalene,
   And St Catharine's, and St John's,
Are the dreariest places,
   And full of dons.

Latin? so slow, so dull an end, lad?
   Oh, that was noble, that was strong!
For you'd a better wit to friend, lad,
   Than many a man who's sung his song.

You'd many a singer's tale to show it,
   Who could not end as he began,
That thirty years eat up a poet,
   And the muse dies before the man.

Such gave the world their best—and quickly
   Poured out that watered best again,
—and age has found them tired and sickly,
   Mouthing youth's flabby dead refrain;—

Or lived on lads whose song's long ended,
   Who will not blush for all they say;
Or damned the younger songs and splendid;
   —Oh, lad, you chose the better way!

Let fools so end! Leave many a lesser
   To blot his easy bettered page!
But play the man, become Professor
   when your ailment is your age!

You turned where no tune yet is clinging,
   Where never a living song was sung;
E'en Greek might tempt a man to singing,
   But Latin is the lifeless tongue.

man' becomes 'And the muse dies before the man.' Brooke's, 'But play the man, become Professor', is a direct reference to Housman's No.45.

This gentle satire, not even a satire really, has no malice in it, just fun, and the joy of parody, with the added spice of hoping to win some money. Brooke had always admired Housman and knew his poetry as a schoolboy and it was not the first time he had parodied him. At the age of 17 he writes to Geoffrey Keynes, ' . . . I can only quote two lines from *The Shropshire Lad* you have often heard upon my lips – a little altered this time. *So dead or living, drunk or dry,/ Keyney, I wish you well!. . .* (No.22).' In 1913 he again parodies Housman (No.13) in a letter to Cathleen Nesbitt when he writes, 'But I'm in San Francisco/ And oh, 'tis true, 'tis true!', and again, in 1915, to Violet Asquith, he writes a parody about ' . . . drowsy drunken seamen'. (Keynes, Letters, p.646)

In 1907 he wrote to Geoffrey Fry, 'I met Laurence Housman the other day. His brother is the only poet in England.' (p.90) Brooke expressed his esteem of Housman in his farewell address to Rugby School's *Eranos* literary society, on his last Sunday as a schoolboy, when he told them there were a few poets who achieved their effects through simplicity – one of them was A.E.Housman. His poems 'did not merit their obscurity'. (Hassall, p.94) Later, at Cambridge, their shared enjoyment of *A Shropshire Lad* is what first brought Brooke and Hugh Dalton together as friends.

In describing Brooke's first meeting with Housman at a dinner at Cambridge, in 1913, Hassall says that Housman was the one man that Brooke had longed for so many years to meet.

Houseman did not publish any more poetry till 1922, so Brooke can only have known the Shropshire Lad poems, and his delightful imitation of them is surely the most sincere flattery.

You may stir that dust to laughter
   The lonely wreath that once you made,
—Unsmirched by feebler song born after—
   We have it where it will not fade.

Those who don't care for song now hear you
   In curious, some in languid, rows.
Undishonoured, clean and clear, you
   Teach and lecture, safe in prose.

For, lads of harsher voice or sweeter,
   They'll all together find one crown,
And hold their tongues from wagging metre
   In this—or in a dustier town.

No lad has made a song-book
   To please the young folks there,
No living tongue is spoken,
   And its little one will care.

And there's time enough to dawdle in,
   And there, there's plenty o' dons,
And its drearier than Magdalene,
   And a long way duller than John's.

1911

Will Ka and Rupert Marry?

Katharine ('Ka') Cox was one of those people to whom everybody turns for help and support, and has been described as a mother figure for Brooke. A student of Newnham College, she became treasurer of the Cambridge Fabians and it was amongst them that he first met her. Although he treated her badly and although he had many different relationships of varying degrees of intensity, Ka remains one of the great loves of Brooke's chaotic love-life.

In 1911 Brooke found himself becoming increasingly attracted to her and that year, immediately after Christmas, they were at Lulworth with a party of friends. Ka was at that time infatuated with the, married, artist Henry Lamb, and had contrived to have him invited to stay near them. Because of this Brooke had a fit of neurotic jealousy which led him into a depression or decline. Losing weight, he was taken to a nerve specialist in Harley Street who recommended that he should go to Cannes where his mother could look after him in a hotel.

Once there he started a series of increasingly frantic letters to Ka imploring her to meet him somewhere in Europe. Eventually he escaped from his mother and met her in Verona, and together they lived in Germany and Austria for three weeks. Ka, still under the spell of Lamb and not really in love with Brooke, apparently gave herself to him as 'therapy'. This uneasy adventure ended with his falling ill again and Ka having to bring him back to England.

Ironically, once Brooke had gained the consummation he sought, he fell out of love with her and Ka fell in love with him. They never resumed their former state of intimacy.

Other loves figure in his life: Noel Olivier, unattainable; Eileen Wellesley, physical; and Cathleen Nesbitt, romantic. But at this time, July 1911, he is obsessed with Ka, and he writes her a letter with this poem in it.

WILL KA AND RUPERT MARRY?

Marriage was on their lips and in their eyes.
Churches they scorned! their hearts unshackled stars
Scurrying, fearless down bewildered skies
To Love's own sanctuary, the Registrar's .
The kind souls trust that 'all will end all right':
'No painful sequel' hope the timid souls:
Two good friends wed is the dear souls' delight.
Not for the game they play, but for the goals.
'Will Ka and Rupert marry? Let us pray!'
If Ka or Rupert loves, they hardly care;
Whose morrows lead to – our least yesterday!
Who pray for day all day, till night is there.
'The Means! How will it *end*?' And all the while
The Eternal End goes by: We love, and smile.

1911

Die Natur

Brooke was a competent gallery critic, who was listened to and published during his lifetime. His interests in art were wide-ranging and he had visited many of the famous art galleries of Europe.

John Lehmann writes 'Rupert's reviews are . . . pithy, trenchant and pertinent . . . It is easy to conceive that he would have become one of the leading critics of his day, and not only of literature but also of the acted play, and even of art, if he had lived and if he had so wanted.' (Lehmann, p.72) He goes on to say that Brooke, while in Germany, had been an eager visitor to exhibitions and came to know the modern continental masters, from Cezanne and Van Gogh onwards.

In the Autumn of 1912, following visits to the second Post-Impressionist Exhibition at the Grafton Galleries, he had written two pieces of criticism for *The Cambridge Magazine* which had shown a wide knowledge of the contemporary artistic scene.

He despised cant and pretentiousness and was always ready to mock shallow social trends. In 1912 Japanese prints were all the rage in London and Brooke would have either overheard or been drawn into chattering over glasses and teacups at fashionable gatherings. He himself became extremely fond of these prints, but the nonsense he had had to listen to had sharpened his wit.

In May 1912 he writes to Noel Olivier, 'I enclose my latest poem. I walked alone two days beyond Potsdam . . . down the lakes. Hence this . . . I'm afraid you won't like the poem . . . ' [1] (Harris, p.178)

---

[1] Pippa Harris notes in *Song of Love* that the poem was published with the title *By the Lake. A Music for three voices*, in *The EyeWitness*, 10 October 1912

DIE NATUR

A lake . . . and then a wood . . .
—That's good, you know, that's good!

The blossom in the trees,
—*Distinctly* Japanese!

White bloom against the sky,
—A perfect Hokusai!

Blue waves and one white spot,
—Sheer Hiroshige, what?

The blue behind the white,
—Oh, delicate! oh, quite!

The white against the blue,
—Artistic, *through and through*!

The plum tree, nicely-placed,
—*That's* what I call good taste.

The rushed bend and bow,
—What price a wood-cut *now*?

The petals on the lake . . .
—That's fony, *no* mistake!

 The petals drift apart —
—Real, high-class, cultured Art!

The petals fade and sink . . .
—Fetches yer, I *don't* think!

1912

Triolet

Frances Darwin was one of the three granddaughters of Charles Darwin who formed part of Brooke's circle at Cambridge. She married Francis Cornford who was a junior classics don at Trinity, and later, as Frances Cornford, became known as a poet.

She and Brooke used to compare notes on their poetry and their writing of poetry. They were firm friends and she, perhaps more than any of his friends, understood him and had a sympathetic appreciation of his character and motives. She it was who wrote the famous quatrain:

> A young Apollo, golden haired
> Stands dreaming on the edge of strife,
> Magnificently unprepared
> For the long littleness of life. (Keynes, Gates, p.156)

Keynes, in his autobiography *The Gates of Memory*, calls it 'her too well-known epigram' and goes on to say, 'She afterwards regretted this kindly-meant tribute, realising how it had trivialised him in the eyes of the world.'

In describing Brooke's approach to writing poetry she had written: 'I can't imagine him using a word of that emotional jargon in which people usually talk or write of poetry. He made it feel more like carpentering.' (Hassall, p.276) He, for his part, used gently to tease her for belonging to a school of poetry which he called the 'Heart-criers, because they believe all poetry ought to be short, simple, naïve & a cry from the heart.' (Keynes, Letters, p.361)

He went on to say, in his letter to Edward Marsh, 'I'm rewriting English Literature on their lines. Do you think this is a fair rendering of Shakespeare's first twenty sonnets if Mrs. Cornford had had the doing of them?' (p.362) And with that he wrote out for Marsh these eight lines headed *Triolet*.

TRIOLET

If you would only have a son,
  William, the day would be a glad one.
It *would* be nice for everyone,
If you would only have a son.
—And, William, what would *you* have done
  If Lady Pembroke hadn't had one?
If you would only have a son,
  William, the day *would* be a glad one.

1912

Hate You?

All who knew Brooke, and all who know his works, agree that most of his work is autobiographical. There is very little textual information about this particular verse, which I have titled from its first line. Hassall has printed it and dated it, and both Hassall and Lehmann point out that in 1912 Brooke was in a paranoid and disturbed frame of mind for some time following the brief, passionate and disastrous episode with Ka Cox.

In the absence of information one can speculate. In this verse he seems to be reflecting on his recent affair with Ka. Frances Cornford is quoted by Hassall: 'his male first conceptions about life were bleeding and broken; he was always re-thinking and always constructing a new universe in the light of his new experiences. Often he was like a man trying lightly to mock at an earthquake which had knocked his house flat.' (Hassall, p.368)

Brooke's view of women is fractured and ambivalent, mediated no doubt by the influence of his puritanical mother, and in the opposite sex he perceives both menace and magnetism, and even real experience leaves him bemused.

'Lilith-Eve' speaks for itself: Lilith the 'night-monster' whom Adam could not subdue, and Eve who seduced him by apple, tree and serpent! Sometimes Brooke blames women – he blamed Ka – and sometimes himself. Now hurt, he withdraws to watch the comedy of life, aloof and alienated. He smiles a faint satirical smile and nurses his injured pride.

Later (January 1913) he writes to Ka:

'Also I know about love. It's all right if one can be taken in enough; and all happens to go happily. But one can't keep it at that. Love *is* being at a person's mercy. And it's a black look-out when the person's an irresponsible modern female virgin. There's no more to say.' (Keynes, Letters, p.417)

HATE YOU?

Hate you? Ah, no! I've much to thank you for,
  —New passion in my latest love-sonnets
A fresh store of exotic epithets,
A novel pose . . . yes, Lilith-Eve[1], and more—
  —You've stayed me with apples—— from the
                                     Knowledge Tree!

  I dreamt. You taught me what the dream was worth.
  I played my part (not clumsily!) Henceforth
I'll sit in the stall and watch the comedy.

Ha! now that hero rants (as I, ere while!)
I like the lad: his soul's one scarlet flame
Lit by Her lips (where lurks your subtle smile!)
In the end they fade and shrivel up and die . . .
We laugh at their brave antics, God and I.

1912

[1] see under 'Lilith' and under 'The Devil and his Dam',
Brewer's Dictionary of Phrase and Fable

There once was a lovely Cathleen

Cathleen Nesbitt records in her autobiography that she first met Rupert Brooke at a dinner party at Eddie Marsh's in December 1912. She told him that one of her favourite poems in Marsh's anthology *Georgian Poetry* was *Heaven* by someone called Rupert Brooke. He blushed scarlet, laughed and said, 'You have very good taste. I wrote *Heaven*, I rather like it myself!'

It is a matter for speculation whether Brooke's love for Cathleen was 'the real love of his life'. (Pearsall, p.41) It competes with the affair with Ka, the long pursuit of the young Noel Olivier, South Seas sex with Taatamata, and sex with others too. Certainly it was the great love of Cathleen's life. About her feelings after his death she wrote, ' . . . I just felt stunned and empty, and a deep anger with myself for not having had a child by him.' (Nesbitt, p.97)

Their love was never consummated; although they used to stay at country inns together they always had separate rooms. She wrote that she couldn't remember when they first realised they were in love; she thought he was aware of it before she was. They shared literary tastes, and the poet John Donne seemed to have infused their dawning love with his verses . . . 'I wonder by my troth what thou and I *did* till we loved?' Once, she records, they lay on a grassy bank and held each other's hands while 'Rupert murmured some lines of Donne's *The Exstasie*.' (p.79)

Soon after Rupert's death she wrote a letter of condolence to Mrs. Brooke on the death of her other son, Alfred[1]. They met after this and became firm friends in their shared love for the man they both had lost. So this love, the most mature of Rupert's life, might have lasted and they might have married, though Cathleen did wonder whether he would have remained faithful.

They often wrote to each other twice a day. He sent her this limerick just before leaving her to go to Canada.

1. in The Kinsman Archive, Temple Reading Room, Rugby School. Published in 'Rupert Brooke's Death and Burial', Imperial War Museum, 1992.

THERE ONCE WAS A LOVELY CATHLEEN

He writes to Cathleen: '. . . . My literary labours haven't been progressing very well. The only complete poem I've produced lately is . . .'

There once was a lovely Cathleen –
I don't think she can ever have been.
It's not *likely*, you know.
P'raps I dreamt it was so.
There aren't *really* such things as Cathleen.

1913

Another time he wrote, just before his return from America: 'I really ought to be able to write more poems about you or to you. I tried one as I lay in bed this morning: . . .'

Cathleen! Loveliest creature! Nymph divine!!
Unhoped for, unapproachable, yet mine!
Fount of all beauty, vision of delight
Whom I love all the day and half the night;
Child, and yet goddess, woman, saint and witch
(rhyme too obvious) . . .

1914

. . . and yet another time – a 'Lovely Cathleen' limerick again [1]

There once was a lovely Cathleen
The loveliest ever was seen
Cleopatra and Helen
And Deirdre I'm tellin' you,
Were not as fair as Cathleen.

There once was a glorious Cathleen
Her face when unswollen and clean
Was so lovely and nice
Quite a face not a fyce
I do enjoy seeing Cathleen.

[1] in *A Little Love and Good Company*, C.Nesbitt, p.87, quoted undated

The Pink and Lily

The *Pink and Lily* was a favourite inn near Princes Risborough and Great Hampden in Buckinghamshire where Brooke used frequently to stay. This poem is difficult to date; it appears in Edward Marsh's *Memoir* in *The Collected Poems*, but he does not give a date. His comment is only that Brooke's English holidays produced 'floods of doggerel' (p.35), and that this particular piece was written on one occasion when he went to the *Pink and Lily* with Jacques Raverat. Keynes, in his autobiography, speculates that he may have written it when he was staying with the poet John Masefield at Pond House at Great Hampden; this was in 1912, but does seem to be only speculation on Keynes part (Keynes himself was living at Pond House in 1942), and nowhere, that I'm aware of, can be found any other reference to when Brooke first discovered this pub, or wrote his poem.

He wrote to Frances Cornford on 20 March 1913 from the *Pink and Lily* and described to her the view: 'The hill drops a few hundred feet in front, and beyond is half Buckinghamshire, Berkshire and Oxfordshire. In this little room is the publican, asleep and rather tipsy.' (Keynes, Letters, p.432) Another letter, to Raverat this time, is dated July 1914 and superscribed 'just back from the Pinque' (*sic*).

Hassall records that in 1913 Brooke took a trip there with Cathleen Nesbitt, and also tells us that on 20 June 1914 he stayed there with Edward Marsh, Ben Keeling and Dudley Ward and that Cathleen joined them for the day. Afterwards Brooke wrote to her of the planning of the second volume of *Georgian Poetry*. Hassall quotes from a letter to her:

'Eddie and I had a perfectly glorious day yesterday; we dissected and discussed and adjudged all the poets with infinite perspicacity and responsibility, and then we walked by those glorious woods to Wendover . . . and drank much beer there . . . and slept in the heather . . . and got back to roast beef and more beer and poems. I wish you had been there.' (Hassall, p.449)

THE PINK AND LILY

Never came there to the Pink
Two such men as we, I think.
Never came there to the Lily
Two men quite so richly silly;
So broad, so supple, and so tall,
So modest and so brave withal,
With hearts so clear, such noble eyes,
Filled with such sage philosophies,
Thirsty for Good, secure of Truth,
Fired by a purer flame than youth,
Serene as age, but not so dirty,
Old, young, mature, being under thirty.
Were ever two so fierce and strong,
Who drank so deep, and laughed so long,
So proudly meek, so humbly proud,
Who walked so far, and sang so loud?

[undated]

The Fleur-de-Lys

As Marsh explained in his *Memoir,* Brooke's English holidays were apt to give rise to doggerel. He tells us that, on one occasion, Brooke and Dudley Ward had come very late to Cranbourne, in Dorset, and couldn't find the inn they had picked out in the guidebook for the sake of its name.

In the evidently inferior Victoria Inn Brooke had passed a sleepless night and during the night had composed this poem, an 'elaborate ballade' about the superior merits of the inn they had been unable to find – probably *imaginary* merits, for history doesn't relate whether Brooke was able to prove by experience that the delights he writes about really existed. Maybe he spent the next night at the Fleur-de-Lys!

Marsh does not tell us the date these verses were written.

THE FLEUR-DE-LYS

In Cranbourne town two inns there are,
  And one the Fleur-de-Lys is hight,
And one, the inn Victoria,
  Where, for it was alone in sight,
  We turned in tired and tearful plight,
Seeking for warmth and company,
  And food, and beds so soft and white –
These things are at the Fleur-de-Lys.

Where is the ointment for the scar?
  Slippers? and table deftly dight?
Sofas? tobacco? soap? and ah!
  Hot water for a weary wight?
  Where is the food, in toil's despite?
The golden eggs? the toast? the tea?
  The maid so pretty and polite?
These things are at the Fleur-de-Lys.

Oh, we have wandered far and far,
  We are foredone and wearied quite.
No lamp is lit; there is no star.
  Only we know that in the night
  We somewhere missed the faces bright,
The lips and eyes we longed to see;
  And Love, and Laughter, and Delight.
These things are at the Fleur-de-Lys.

Prince, it is dark to left and right,
  Waits there an inn for you and me?
Fine noppy ale and red firelight?
  These things are at the Fleur-de-Lys.

[undated]

Motoring

Eric Gill, sculptor, typographer, artist, writer, wood-engraver, printer and publisher, lived in a kind of artistic commune at Ditchling Common in Sussex. He was a friend of both Brooke and Geoffrey Keynes. He was an all-round craftsman with a uniquely evolving style in his sculpture that Brooke much admired, as did Keynes. After Brooke's death it was Gill who executed the incised lettering of the sonnet *The Soldier* which is inscribed on his memorial plaque in Rugby School Chapel. (see page 98)

Brooke was keen on acquiring a small *Madonna and Child*, for which Gill had 'done an extraordinarily good cast for a bronze'. (Keynes, Letters, p.416) He wanted Keynes – and others – to buy more copies of the statuette in order to cheapen the price. He did buy a copy and sent it to Edward Marsh to keep for Ka Cox, as a parting gift. She was at that time in Germany and he was about to embark for America. He eventually wrote and told her about it in a sort of 'final-and-farewell' letter written from New York on 29 June 1913.

Earlier, in January of the same year, he is writing to Keynes happily anticipating a motor trip by a 'party of (*secretly*) prospective purchasers' – himself, Keynes, Edward Marsh and Justin Brooke – to Ditchling to buy the bronze. He suggests that they should go one Saturday or Sunday and that 'Eddie' should stand lunch ('don't tell him.'); however the accompanying poem in the letter seems to suggest that it should be a picnic!

In this letter (written from Cornwall) he tells Keynes that he has written nothing for months except a fragment which he called *Motoring*; 'It went on a long time', he adds, 'but I omitted to write it down: & have forgotten it.'

MOTORING

The part of motoring *I* like,
Is luncheon near the Devil's Dyke.
—The country's really very fair,
From beyond Ditchling Beacon there:
The view is very *sweet*, and very
Pretty, from there to Chanctonbury:
But still, the part of it *I* like
Is luncheon near the Devil's Dyke.
            . . .   .

Chicken & sausage-roll laid out,
Pudding, and stout, oh Jesus, *stout!*.
            . . .   .

Above my head the clouds they pass;
My table-cloth is the green grass.
            . . .   .

My mouth is covered with stout-froth –
The green grass is my table-cloth.

1913

The Hills of Heaven

In April 1913 Brooke wrote to his two artist friends, Jaques and Gwen Raverat. Addressing them as 'Dear Children liebe Kinder', he wrote them a goodbye letter on the verge of his taking ship to New York – he eventually embarked on May 22. In it he explained that he would not be coming to see them before he went away, excusing himself because he had so much to do. (Keynes, Letters, p.456)

He was writing from 5 Thurloe Square, which, as Hassall explains, was a flat which he had taken so as to give another and more needy poet a chance of Marsh's spare room – this was the room at his Grays Inn home that Edward Marsh had put at Brooke's disposal.

It was Naomi Royde Smith, the literary editor of *The Westminster Gazette*, who had heard that Brooke wanted to travel, and had made an offer of an expenses-paid trip to North America to write travel articles for her paper at a fee of four guineas each.

Making preparations for his long absence, he explained to the Raverats that he would have to go to Rugby, 'to pacify a bitter and enraged Ranee'[1]. "The Ranee", his mother, would find the intended parting a wrench.

Perhaps, whimsically, he suggested if he and the Raverats didn't meet again in this world, they might only find each other 'in a whiter world, nighty-clad, harped, winged, celibate – oh, dear, oh, dear!'. Nostalgically he thinks of those recent years when, as the 'dew dabblers', they roamed the English countryside together.

Roaming the hills of Heaven, this verse suggests, might be all that's left to them if they never meet again on this earth. 'No: let us not die.' – he firmly adds, jerking himself back from this poetic fantasy.

---

[1] Friends at Cambridge had suggested a (non-existent) family relationship with Brooke the White Rajah of Sarawak. So the title of *The Ranee* was conferred on Rupert's mother: he thought it fitting and used it frequently.

THE HILLS OF HE

Shall we go walks along the hills of He
—Rucksack on back and aureole in pocke
And stay in Paradisal pubs, and drink
Immortal toasts in old Ambrosia,
Fry wings in nectar on the glassy sea,
And build the fire with twigs of amaranth.

1913

ur of North America he took with
e of the actress Cathleen Nesbitt,
He was in love with her – at least it
t and foreground of his polygamous
en continually filled with romantic
she had anticipated, entirely faithful
l with feelings of longing for her.

persuade Cathleen not to take up an
s. He himself embarked in May 1913,
ordinary letter pleading with her not to
go to America saying.

' . . . you'd understand how desperately frightened and miserable I become at the thought of you going away . . . Dear love, I *daren't* go wandering. You don't know what a helpless poor fool I am. It's only in love and marriage I can find peace.' (Keynes, Letters, pp.450-51)

And yet a few days later he wrote and said:

'It gets worse, I find. I do love you so: and yet I'm going to leave England in May. I've got to go, for a bit. Because I promised. I got mixed up with a woman[1]. Do you know how human beings tear each other? I've been so torn, and torn so.' (p.455)

His attempt to stop her going was typical of the double standards of Brooke's Victorian male mind.

As soon as he had embarked on the *S.S.Cedric*, on 23 May, he found a letter from her waiting. Overjoyed he writes, 'My darling you give me so much more than I deserve.' (p.462) He had just eaten clam chowder – so he goes on to send her this clever amorous little poem.

[1] Katharine Cox

CLAM CHOWDER

If you were like Clam Chowder,
   And I were like the spoon,
And the band was playing louder
   And a little more in tune,

I'd stir you till I spilled you,
   Or I'd kiss you till I killed you,
If you were like Clam Chowder
   And I were like the spoon.

1913

Homesickness – 'Nostalgia'
1. Cauliflowers 2. Across the Sea

Although Brooke travelled extensively in Europe and – presumably willingly – had accepted an offer from *The Westminster Gazette* of a commission to travel in the New World, and supply them with travel pieces, he nevertheless became frequently a prey to homesickness.

When he left England for New York he went, steered into the project by Frances Cornford's insistence, to effect his mental rehabilitation after the ill-starred affair with Katharine Cox. Mrs. Cornford had said, 'I believe the point of going so far is to forget us all, like a deep sleep.' (Hassall, p.395) He was persuaded to go, he was content to go, but it was inevitable that he should, from time to time, feel loneliness and a nostalgia for friends and familiar places.

Brooke had a love of the places and scenery, and the towns and villages of England, that was intense and personal and part of his poetic appetite – an appetite that needed to be fed with fresh English journeys and experiences. When out of England he yearned to be back there. *The Old Vicarage, Grantchester,* was written in a Berlin café, and interwoven with its humour is this deep love of a locality where he longs to be, in this case Cambridgeshire. He also wrote of Warwickshire, 'But it is lovely. It's the sort of country I adore. I'm a Warwickshire man.' (Keynes, Letters, p.599)

As is usual with Brooke, there is such flippancy in these two quatrains that one cannot be sure how deep the homesickness goes. By now he is under the spell of Cathleen Nesbitt and, on arrival in New York he writes to her, 'I'm crying. I want you. I don't want to be alone.' (p.468) In the letter which contains *Cauliflowers* Brooke thanks Geoffrey Keynes for coming to his farewell 'Bierundgerösteteschweinfleischlebwohlnehmengesellschaft', and tells him with an air of wonder that he had '*Clam Chowder*' for dinner.

To Keynes he writes from the ship, 'I've already begun an interminable series of poems about England entitled *Nostalgia*.' (p.467) and to the Raverats, on a postcard from Boston dated 21st June, 'Good people, good people: I am homesick once a week, for an hour; and this is the hour this week. Pray for me.' (p.473)

CAULIFLOWERS

In England oh the cauliflowers
They blow through all the English hours,
And all New York's clam chowder is
Less dear than Rugby strawberries.

1913

ACROSS THE SEA

Across the sea, Across the sea,
My heart goes out to J. and G:
All the way, from Americay,
My heart goes out to G. and J.

1913

To Cathleen Nesbitt

The relationship between Rupert Brooke and Cathleen Nesbitt has already been discussed (page 70). In her autobiography, *A Little Love and Good Company*, she quotes (p.87) six lines which she implies he wrote just before his return from America in 1914. However in *The Letters* appears a poem of sixteen lines containing the same six lines and dated 25 June 1913.

The letter starts with the poem, and ends:

'Oh, dear, I'm so sorry. I've a sort of feeling that I'm a poet and ought to write to my beloved in verse; for then it'll come out in my *Life and Letters*, and be printed in an Appendix to my collected works, and they'll all say 'How wonderful to write letters in verse! and how beautiful she must have been!' . . .

But it's no good. For I cannot say half the things I want to. I have to drop into mere prose; where there's a larger stock of words to praise you in.' (Keynes, Letters, p.474)

Nesbitt's account in her book is similar to the letter referred to above, except that part of it appears to be paraphrased. *The Letters* were published in 1967 and her biography in 1975. Obviously she must have let Keynes have many of her letters for publication and presumably have received them back; one assumes she would have had this letter before her when she wrote her book. Keynes is known to have been inaccurate over his dating of many of Brooke's letters, and in *The Letters* the year '1913' is written in square brackets, which means that Brooke in writing the date had not included the year and Keynes had guessed it. One can only suggest that readers compare the two works.

TO CATHLEEN NESBITT

Now the hot labour of the day is done
How nice it is to lie with nothing on
Except a thin, a yellow dressing gown,
And listen to the noises of the town,
And think of what I've done and where I've been
And write a letter to my dear Cathleen.
Cathleen! loveliest creature! nymph divine!
Unhoped for, unapproachable, yet mine!
Fount of all beauty, vision of delight,
Whom I love all the day and half the night;
Child, and yet goddess, woman, saint and witch
(Rhyme too obvious –)
Perplexing compound, teasing wonderment,
Wiser than God, and baby-innocent,
Sweeter than love, and bitterer than death,
Lucrezia Helen Mary in a breath.

1913

Brooke had many friends and had – or had passed through – several different circles of friends. First there had been his Cambridge friends, and in particular that close circle known as the 'dew-dabblers' from their habit of walking, camping and picnicking. Then there had been a loose association with the Bloomsbury group, including Virginia Woolf and the Stracheys – from whom, having quarrelled with the Stracheys, he had subsequently distanced himself. Finally, by 1912, there was the artistic and fashionable London world to which Edward Marsh had introduced him.

Marsh first met Brooke at Cambridge and, having seen him in 1906 playing the Herald in *The Eumenides* of Aeschylus, experienced, as Delany says, a *coup de foudre* at his first sight of Rupert's 'radiant youthful figure'. (Delaney, p.20) In September 1912 'Eddie' had offered him a permanent pied-a-terre at his flat at Gray's Inn.

Marsh, who was private secretary to Winston Churchill, was a cultivated man and an influential patron of the arts, and from then on Brooke moved in exalted circles, eventually becoming accepted as a friend of the Prime Minister's family – in particular forming a firm friendship with Violet Asquith. He and Marsh had been guests at her birthday dinner at 10 Downing Street, and it was there that he had eaten plover's eggs and sat among all these distinguished people. Overcome once again by nostalgia he reminisces about it to Marsh, from Ottawa, in a short verse which, if uttered to anyone else, could have been accounted shameless name-dropping.

However, Brooke, as usual, is gently self-mocking and writes: 'I make up little minor pitiful songs, the burden of which is that I have a folk-longing to get back from all this Imperial luxury to the simplicity of the little places and quiet folks I knew & loved'. (Keynes, Letters, p.482) Quiet simplicity is hardly a feature of the exalted company he misses!

PLOVER'S EGGS

Would God I were eating Plover's Eggs,
  And drinking dry champagne,
With the Bernard Shaws, Mr and Mrs Masefield,
Lady Horner, Neil Primrose, Raleigh, the Right
Honourable Augustine Birrell, Eddie, six or
  seven Asquiths, & Felicity Tree,
In Downing Street again.

1913

King's

In a letter to A.F.Scholfield, from Toronto, Brooke is once again expressing that homesickness which he calls '*heimweh*'– 'I drip horribly with *Heimweh*, nearly the whole time. Don't you? I have the advantage (?) that I can write – and do – vast quantities of nostic verse . . . ' (Keynes, Letters, p.490)

The reason Brooke asks Scholfield whether he also suffers from home-sickness is because he had, the previous year, taken up an appointment in India, where he was living at the time of Brooke's letter. In September 1912 Brooke had written to Scholfield saying, 'I am considerably perturbed that the Empire has claimed you. Shan't we see you for years?' (p.404)

Rupert Brooke and Scholfield had first met at King's College, Cambridge. Brooke was a freshman and Scholfield, who was in his fourth year, was a leading light in the production of plays and had first spotted Brooke at a rehearsal of *Eumenides*. Being struck by his good looks, he asked to be introduced and wondered whether he might help with the play. Justin Brooke, who had explained that they were not related, said, 'You won't get much out of him, he's very shy.' (Hassall, 106) So it was that Rupert came to play the non-speaking part of the Herald. It could be said that he was a visual success!

Later they became firm friends and often dined and went to shows together. In 1909, just before he went to Grantchester to live, Brooke wrote to 'Scho', as he called him, to decline the idea of their sharing college rooms, saying he would like nothing better except that he desired solitude, and add-ing 'I passionately long to shut myself wholly up and read only and always.' (Keynes, Letters, p.171)

In 1913, envisaging him as a fellow exile and writing from Canada, Brooke no doubt felt Scholfield would share his nostalgia for 'King's'.

KING'S

My heart is sick for several things
Only to be found in King's . . .

I do recall those haunts with tears,
The Backs, the Chapel, and the Rears . . .

O Places of perpetual mire,
Localities of my desire,
O lovely, O remembered gloom
And froust of Chetwynd lecture-room,
Dear haunts with old romance aglow
Where first I viewed the passing *show.*   [paronomasia]
O spots my memory yet is gilding,
O Jumbo Arch! O Wilkins Building!

.   .   .

[descriptive of
the Natural
Beauties]

Ah, how my memory floods and fills,
The Hills[1] and Brookes[2] and little Sills!
The Olive and other greenery[3]
And Canes complete the scenery:
And, in my dream, stretch far away
Montes et Knox perpetua . . .

(1) A.V. and W.D.P.
(2) R.C., A.C. & A.E.
(3) e.g. The Birch.

[The poet, to
hide his
emotion, drops
into latin]

There we pursued the truth amain,
With Dialectic and Champagne,
And, through the young and purple night,
Still holla'd after 'What is Right',
And played the young philosopher
From Hesperus till Lucifer,
And stalked and startled from her nest
The subtle bird, *quod verum est,*
And linked with the new risen sun,
To kalon with To agaqon

89

Rupert Brooke in 1913

Photograph by Scherrill Schell
National Portrait Gallery

(but this is getting bawdy: and the rhymes aren't all your pedantic
ear would wish; besides, you're laughing at my accents. I know
you! German! Yah! So all End, all End!)

Dear Home of my Rememberings!
O King's! O King's! O King's! O King's!

(my style when
they pay me by
space)

Spot where I cheered the College Bumps,

(not I! 'tis but
for the rhyme)

Place where I read First Less'n in pumps!
Founded the New Jerusalem!
And breakfasted at 3 p.m!
Haunts where I drank the whole damn night!
Place where I catted till the light!
Dear spot where I was taken short,
O Bodley's Court! O Bodley's Court!

(with Schloss,
Reitlinger, etc.,
etc.)

1913

Ligature

In September 1913 Brooke wrote, from Vancouver, to Edward Marsh, who had sprained his ankle, 'I got your letter of August 26th. just now; from the bed of pain. Isn't ligature – or is it ligament? – a lovely word?' (Keynes, *Letters*, p.507), and then proceeds to entertain him with this nonsense verse. It is to be hoped that Marsh was no longer on 'the bed of pain' when he received his friend's letter and was able to laugh at it.

Rupert Brooke was always fascinated by words; he would often be exploring meanings and using, sometimes, unusual words purely for effect. In his poems he would often leave blanks until just the right word occurred to him. In this case he is simply playing with two like sounding words, happily oblivious of the fact (or is he?) that the word 'ligature' represents no tissue that occurs naturally in the human body.

Geoffrey Keynes, in editing *The Letters of Rupert Brooke*, and having by that time become 'Sir Geoffrey', the famous surgeon, states in a footnote that it was on account of the sprained ankle that Edward Marsh became his *first* private patient. He doesn't state whether, being a friend, he charged a fee! At twenty-six he had yet to make a name for himself. Any fee would have been rather less than he was able to charge from Harley Street many years later.

In the meantime Rupert, being thousands of miles from the clinical concerns of his two friends, waxes lyrical over the 'lovely' medical words, saying, 'Oh, it sets one singing'!

LIGATURE

'Is it prudent? is it pure?
To go & break a ligature?'
'With lissom ligament
My lovely one she went
   And trod the street
   On quiet feet'—
'Torn, like a ligament, his random mind' . . .

1913

Princess Angeline

Noel Olivier was the first love of Rupert Brooke's life. They met in 1908 when she was fifteen and he was twenty. This was at a Cambridge Fabian supper party when he went to help her and cover her embarrassment over a broken and spilt cup of coffee. Her father, Sir Sydney Olivier, an ex-Governor of Jamaica, had been invited to address the group, and she was the youngest there – she must have been feeling very shy, and no doubt grateful to the susceptible Rupert, for whom it seems to have been love at first sight.

She subsequently took up a medical career and became a consultant paediatrician. She married another doctor, a GP, and had five children. During her lifetime (she died aged 76) she steadfastly refused to allow publication of any of her correspondence with Brooke, and it was not until 1991 that her granddaughter, Pippa Harris, published this correspondence as a book entitled *Song of Love*. To quote from its dust-jacket: ' . . . (he) began to bombard her with highly charged and exuberant letters . . . Despite her youth, Noel held her own in the face of the poet's romantic onslaught, replying with painstaking honesty and astonishing verve.'

In the preface to the same work is quoted an excerpt from Virginia Woolf's diary, where she asks Noel why she didn't marry any of those 'romantic young men', to which she had replied:

'She didn't know, said she had moods . . . And Rupert had gone with Cathleen Nesbitt & she had been jealous, & he had spoken against women & gone among the Asquiths & changed. But when she read his love letter—beautiful beautiful love letters—real love letters, she said—she cries & cries.'

One gets the impression that she did indeed hold him at arm's length, and put her career before getting involved in a love affair. Brooke sent this poem to her from California on a postcard dated 16 September 1913.

PRINCESS ANGELINE

[Postcard 'from somewhere in the Sierra Nevada']

1

Of beauteous dames of noble birth,
Many, thank God, shall walk the earth:
And many fair as stars have been;
But none like Princess Angeline.

2

For Deirdre men have suffered Hell;
And some loved Helen all too well,
And Cleopatra, that dark queen;
I loved the Princess Angeline.

3

Keats hymned his Fanny (more fool he!),
And Browning sang of Mrs B.
And Longfellow, Evangeline.
I sing the Princess Angeline.

4

Shout to the sackbut, shrill the flute!
Whisper it low upon the lute!
Strike loud, strike loud, the tambourine!
I love the Princess Angeline.

5

Some like 'em young: & like 'em pretty,
Winsome & round & red & witty:
They love a pert & plumpy quean,
And tend to find *my* angel lean.

6

Some love a love divine, & bow
To white hands, & an ivory brow
And pale unmoved immortal mien;
And mock the earthy Angeline.

7

But laughter's better than loveliness,
And wrinkled cheeks than youth, I guess,
A gay heart than soul serene,
—*So I stick to Princess Angeline.*

one could go on forever–Rupert

1913

95

A Letter to Violet Asquith
1. A Savage's Delight 2. I know an Island

Keynes, in the 'Biographical Preface 1913', of *The Letters*, notes two facts: that Brooke had finally succeeded in becoming a Fellow of King's College and also that he met, for the first time, Violet Asquith, afterwards Lady Violet Bonham Carter, a daughter of the Prime Minister. (Keynes, Letters, p.413)

The two events were connected: during February and March of that year he was staying with Edward Marsh in Gray's Inn, and it was there on the 8th of March that he received the news of his election to the Fellowship, and there that, three days later, Marsh gave a dinner party that became a celebration of Brooke's achievement. It was at this dinner that he met the two daughters of Herbert Asquith, Cynthia and Violet. This was to be the beginning of a friendship with Violet, marked by a sincere mutual esteem, and one which – as Keynes says – gave rise to some of Brooke's most witty letters.

Violet Asquith was the last person to see Rupert Brooke alive on English soil, for she saw him off for Gallipoli, together with her brother Arthur ('Oc') on the troopship *Grantully Castle* at Avonmouth on 27 February 1915. The two men were serving in the Hood Battalion of Churchill's Royal Naval Division. In her memoir, *Winston Churchill as I Knew Him*, she says, 'I saw in his eyes that he felt sure we should never see each other again.'

His first letter to her, addressed formally, 'Dear Miss Asquith', and written in mid-December 1913 from 'Somewhere in the mountains of Fiji,' (Keynes, Letters, p.540) is long and entertaining and contains two poems: one a witty rumination about one's loved-one being eaten by cannibals (cannibalism had been a common practice in Fiji some twenty years previously), and the other, a lyrical piece about a South Sea island.

A SAVAGE'S DELIGHT

The limbs that erstwhile charmed your sight,
Are now a savage's delight;
The ear that heard your whispered vow
Is one of many *entrées* now;
Broiled are the arms in which you clung
And devilled is the angelic tongue; . . .
And oh! my anguish as I see
A Black Man gnaw your favourite knee!
Of the two eyes that were your ruin,
One now observes the other stewing.
My lips (the inconstancy of man!)
Are yours no more. The legs that ran
Each dewy morn their love to wake,
Are now a steak, are now a steak! . . .

Oh, dear! I suppose it ought to end on the Higher Note, the Wider Outlook. Poetry has to, they tell me. You may caress details all the main part of the poem, but at last you have to open the window – turn to God, or Earth, or Eternity, or any of the Grand Old Endings. It gives Uplift, as we Americans say. And that's so essential. (Did you ever notice how the Browning family's poems *all* refer suddenly to God in the last line. It's laughable if you read through them in that way. 'What if that friend happened to be – God?', 'What comes next – is it God?', 'And with God be the rest', 'And if God choose, I shall but love thee better after death' – etc. etc. I forget them all, now. It shows what the Victorians were.) So I must soar –

O love, O loveliest and best,
Natives this *body* may digest,
Whole, and still yours, my *soul* shall dwell,
Unseen, safe, incoctible.

Memorial plaque in Rugby College Chapel by James Havard Thomas   *National Portrait Gallery*

I KNOW AN ISLAND

I know an Island,
Where the long scented holy nights pass slow,
And there, twixt lowland and highland,
The white stream falls into a pool I know,
Deep, hidden with ferns and flowers , soft as dreaming,
Where the brown laughing dancing bathers go.

it ends, after many pages

I know an Island,
Where the slow fragrant-breathing nights creep past,
And then, twixt lowland and highland,
A deep, fern-shrouded murmurous water glimmers;
There I'll come back at last,
And find my friends, the flower-crowned laughing
swimmers
And . . .

1913

Chislehurst

Frances Cornford, the poet and friend and confidante of Brooke, had suffered from depression and in her teens had suffered episodes of nervous breakdown. According to Delany she had remained 'emotionally fragile' (p.221) and had had, at various periods of her life, to spend time undergoing cures for her mental state.

Evidently one of these cures, in 1914, must have been at Chislehurst, for Brooke wrote her a postcard, dated 15 June, saying 'I'm awfully glad you're better. It sounds a lovely way of being cured.' (Keynes, Letters, p.593) This refers to treatment by 'suggestion' to which she submitted for a short time.

Brooke himself had suffered depressive illness, at the time of the Lulworth episode, so he goes on to say, 'I wish I'd tried it in the old days. It's made me start a poem for you –'. Hence the quatrain on the postcard.

He continued this postcard by saying that he wanted very much to come to Cley, which sounded lovely. It was the home of the Cornfords and, in fact, he did go there to stay with them, on the very day that war was declared with Germany.

CHISLEHURST

The world may go from worse to worst
I shall recline at Chislehurst
And in a neuropathic attitude
Feed my subconscious with platitude.

1914

A-metrist of Anerley

Two disparate figures, Taatamata and Walter de la Mare, find a place in this commentary on an odd little limerick, which appears in a letter to Edward Marsh written from Tahiti in March 1914.

First, Taatamata: she gets a mention because the letter is headed 'Tahiti still', and possibly – because she hasn't been mentioned previously in this work. Keynes his 'Biographical Preface, 1914', says, 'He had lost his heart to a girl called Taatamata' and records that Brooke prolonged his stay in Tahiti for over three months before returning to North America and continuing his travels. (Keynes, Letters, p.557) The reason he prolonged his stay is obvious.

She was the daughter of a village chief, the 'Mamua' to whom the poem *Tiare Tahiti* was addressed. She is described by Hassall as 'a native girl of rare grace and intelligence' (Hassall. p.431) and wrote a famously touching letter to Brooke after he had left the island, which some believe just hints that he may have left her pregnant – 'I get fat all time Sweetheart.' (Keynes, Letters, p.653) Recent evidence has come to light suggesting that Taatamata did in fact have a daughter, of whom Brooke was the father, and that this daughter is only very recently deceased.

As to Walter de la Mare, he lived at Anerley and was a great friend of Brooke. Planning his return to England, Brooke wrote to Marsh anticipating that he would go to Anerley and see de la Mare. In this rhyme he is apparently criticising his fellow poet's metre. Certainly not an 'a-metrist' himself, he feels that anapaests and spondees are intrusive and difficult to handle in English poetry.

De la Mare was one of three poets who received a third share of Rupert Brooke's royalties after his death. The other two were Wilfrid Gibson and Lascelles Abercrombie. Brooke had written, 'If I can set them free, to any extent, to write the poetry and plays and books they want to, my death will bring more gain than loss.' (Hassall, p.517) De la Mare wrote criticisms of Brooke's work, and in 1919, delivered at Rugby School a memorial address entitled *Rupert Brooke and the Intellectual Imagination*.

A-METRIST OF ANERLEY

There once was an a-metrist of Anerley,
Whose neighbours were mundane but mannerly,
  They don't cavil the least
  At a stray anapaest,
But they *do* bar his spondees in Anerley.

1914

The Snail

In Hassall's *Biography* we read that it was during a visit to his grandfather's in Bournemouth in 1896 that the young Rupert Brooke first discovered poetry, in the form of the works of Robert Browning, and that 'the shock was profound'. (Hassall p.28)

Whatever this may mean, Browning's was the first poetry that he read as a child and Browning remained one of the dominating influences in Brooke's development as a poet. Hints of Browning and his way with words appear scattered throughout Brooke's works.

Browning's ideas and utterance had been new in English poetry and people considered him difficult. In 1912, the centenary of Browning's birth, in an article on the poet, Brooke had written, 'It became a favourite pastime for ingenious brains to construe the craggiest passages in Browning, and to read him was for long in England the mark of a taste for nimble intellectual exercise rather than for a love of poetry.' (p.536) Nevertheless Brooke retained a sympathy with Browning which marked his own poetry. He had read him extensively and Hassall records that, in his student days, he had 'ploughed through Sordello' – all 5000 lines of it! (p.97)

Keynes notes (Letters, p.594) that the snatch of rhyme included in a letter to Jacques Raverat (July 1914 – 'just back from the Pinque') is a parody of a passage in Browning's *Pippa Passes*. The original is thus:

[from without is heard the voice of Pippa singing –

... The hill-side's dew-pearled;

The lark's on the wing;
The snail's on the thorn:
God's in his heaven –
All's right with the world!

'The Dud' is Brooke's friend Dudley Ward, and of course Strachey, as the snail, epitomises Brooke's developed, almost paranoid, dislike of the latter.

THE SNAIL

Cheero!
The snail (= Lytton Strachey)'s on the Thorn:
(& may he stay There):
The afternoon is dew-pearled:
The Dud is in London
All's right with the World!
Cheeroh!

1914

Two Artists

The two artists Brooke referred to in this limerick were Jacques and Gwen Raverat. They were amongst the closest friends of his Cambridge days. They had married in 1910. As is so often evident in his letters, Brooke was envious of his married friends, the Cornfords, the Dudley Wards, the Raverats. He had this intense curiosity about what it was like being married; he gave the impression that he felt excluded – looking in enviously from outside. He had a strongly expressed desire to be married, he felt he needed to be, but could not decide to whom. He starts this letter to Gwen with a seemingly envious remark, whose purport is a little obscure because he explains it no further, 'Life is extraordinarily easy for married people isn't it?' (Keynes, Letters, p.600)

The letter is about meeting them in London and is full of Brookeisms, half-meant, half-joking. He does not want to meet them at a restaurant in Soho, ' . . . those very dirty little places, established by the Latin races, and frequented by would-be Bohemians . . . Soho makes me sick so does Mongolian music. I *do* think you're degraded.' He will join them at listening to Asiatic music but says he's not keen. Besides, he might find himself sitting next to a 'Str-ch-y' – the old, and now habitual, animosity towards the Stracheys declares itself yet again.

This was a period in his life of hectic sociability among the gilded and the talented; he was constantly making new friends, among artists as well as writers. In the letter he mentions Stanley Spencer whom he calls 'Cookham', after the artist's home town. The very next letter in *The Letters* begins 'Dear Cookham' and tells Spencer what a wonderful time he had had with Jacques and Gwen in London.

At this time Brooke was restlessly anticipating and worrying about the coming war, and Hassall says that his 'light-hearted sociability had become a facade behind which he smouldered.' (p.452)

TWO ARTISTS

There once were two Artists said 'Ho!
Let us Go, and eat Dirt, in Soho!
  Et aprés ça, allez,
  Ze Mongolian Ballet!
O, *aren't* we Bohemian, O!'

1914

Drunken Seamen

Any stoker, back in 1914, might have told a casual enquirer that stokers were the backbone of the Navy, for the simple reason that, without them, slaving away in the dim light of the roaring stokeholds below the water-line, the ships could not put to sea. Simple-minded chaps, often looked down on by the upper-deck men, they were nevertheless proud of the job they did.

How surprised they must have been when they found themselves turned into soldiers and put into khaki. These same simple-minded chaps were to fight with extreme heroism, in Churchill's Royal Naval Division at Gallipoli and on the Western Front. It is not immediately clear, though historians may understand it, how so many stokers were found to be surplus and combed out of the sea-going Navy to fight on land. However this was Churchill's master plan, and Brooke, on joining the RND as a sub-lieutenant, found his platoon was composed almost entirely of stokers.

A letter to Violet Asquith, (Keynes, Letters, p.646) postmarked 26 December 1914, from the Hood Battalion, 2nd Naval Brigade, Blandford, where Brooke and his stokers were in training, tells her of his fascinating discovery that their camp is on the site of a *Roman* (his italics) camp.

He writes:

> Half my stokers are dancing half-naked in their huts. They spent the night on cheap gin. The surrounding woods are full of lost and sleeping stokers. I expect most of them froze over-night. Pathetic creatures.

He continues:

> I gave my platoon the slip yesterday morning (they were out gathering holly) and went a delicious country walk, decanting drops of a poem (don't report me).

He then includes these two quatrains, which Keynes suggested was another of his parodies of Housman – an apt thought, though there is no obvious point-of-reference in the Housman canon.

DRUNKEN SEAMEN

And drowsy drunken seamen
   Straying belated home,
Meet with a Latin challenge,
   From sentinels of Rome—

In dreams they doff their khaki,
   Put greaves and breastplates on:
In dreams each leading stoker,
   Turns a centurion—, etc . . .

1914

Shipboard Songs

On his return journey to America, at the end of his travels, Brooke had been introduced by letter to Maurice Browne by Harold Monro, who was his brother-in-law. Browne was an Englishman who owned the Little Theatre in Chicago. His wife was the actress Ellen Van Volkenberg, who later played The Daughter in Brooke's one-act play *Lithuania*.

The meeting with Browne and his circle had been an instant success and Brooke spent ten enjoyable days with them. Browne wrote '. . . in the course of those ten days we made him read us almost everything he had written, including *Lithuania*, and all the South Sea poems.' (p.15)

Lithuania was the only play Brooke wrote for performance in the theatre. Browne was the first person to stage it, in his Chicago theatre in 1915 shortly after Brooke's death, and it has not been staged more than half-a-dozen times since. The play leads on from the moment when a long-lost son returns to his peasant family determined to surprise and benefit them with the fortune that he has made; he is not recognised; they give him a bed and he decides to reveal himself to them in the morning, but in the night he is murdered by his own sister for his money and gold watch.

Brooke got on so well with the Brownes that, having learned that they intended to travel to England, he persuaded them to go with him, and together the three of them embarked on the *S.S. Philadelphia* on 29 May 1914. On this voyage they were joined by Ronald Hargreave the painter, and the four of them spent their time mainly playing bridge and competing with each other in composing amusing sonnets and rhymes.

Ellen Van Volkenberg, in her diary of the voyage, wrote, (Browne, p.28) 'There is a concert in progress in the dining saloon, where the thirty Glee Club Boys from California are singing to all the multitude except Rupert Brooke, Don[1] and myself. We are sitting in magnificent and lonely state in the library writing such exquisite ballads as this and drinking beer and lemonade.' In describing the 'immortal sonnets' they wrote she says that Mr. Hargreave was so ashamed of his that he threw it overboard . . . and again: (p.31) 'Here's a "threnody" for Mr. Hargreave that Mr. Brooke has just written; the steward came up and solemnly gave Mr. B. a note from Mr. H., in which he (Mr. H.) said that he was so ashamed of his sonnet that he had jumped overboard.

. . . And so these few flippant rhymes truly became 'immortal'!

[1] Maurice Browne

SING NOT OF CALIFORNIA

Sing not of California, no!
Nor of nothin' else, O woe!
Damn you, be dumb.
For some, God wot, have voices rare: but some
Know not when golden silence should
Sink like a drowsy bird within the wood,
That twitters once, before the night, and then,
Head under wing, leans up against his hen
And shoves her off the branch. They hush their laughter..
So silence follows song, and sleep comes after –
Sleep of the evening: would that it came faster!
(again she sings: God blast her).

1914

Browne notes: '. . . The 1st, 4th, 7th and 10th lines were by Brooke and are in his handwriting; the 2nd, 5th, 8th and 11th were by Miss Van Volkenberg, the 3rd, 6th, 9th and 12th by me. The rest of these otherwise immortal poems - there must have been a dozen or more - died (fortunately) at birth.'

THRENODY

The world's great painter-soul, whom we deplore,
Loved California much, but music more.
His verse – but hush! the poor man's dead and gone.
What Fifi[1] lost the mermaidens have won.

1914

[1] *Fifi* was Brooke's nickname for one of the girls on board.

Dysentery

This little rhyme is the last bit of known and recorded comic verse that Brooke ever wrote. In Egypt he had fallen ill with dysentery and, running a high temperature, had lain outside his tent, under an awning. Here he had been visited by the C-in-C, Sir Ian Hamilton who, on 2nd April 1915, had come to review the Naval Division.

The C-in-C, who had met Brooke in London, sat by his bed and talked poetry with him. He was already anxious about him and offered him a position on his staff. Brooke refused, saying he would rather see the Gallipoli adventure through with his own men.

That same day, still with a raging fever, he got up and went by cab to join his brother-officer, Patrick Shaw-Stewart, also lying sick with dysentery, at the Casino Palace Hotel at Port Said. There an extra bed was put up for Brooke and for several days the two men lay side by side, weak and ill. In this verse the uncomfortable and compelling urges of dysentery are comically treated, but tragically this was in effect Brooke's last illness – in three weeks he was dead.

Still in a weakened condition, he and Shaw-Stewart boarded their troop-ship, the *Grantully Castle*, on 9th April and set sail for Lemnos, where the Gallipoli invasion fleet was being assembled. At that time he had a swelling on his upper lip from a mosquito bite; it subsided, but later swelled up again and caused the septicaemia from which, in a hospital ship, he died on 23rd April. He was buried on the island of Skyros.

As he lay dying, news came that Dean Inge had read Brooke's sonnet *The Soldier*, in conjunction with a text from Isaiah, from the pulpit of St. Paul's on Easter Sunday. The Dean, in commenting on its nobility of expression, had said however that it fell short of Christian hope and of Isaiah's vision. Joking to the last, Brooke murmured that he was sorry Inge didn't think he was as good as Isaiah.

DYSENTERY

My first was in the night, at 1,
At half-past 5 I had to run,
  At 8.15 I fairly flew;
At noon a swift compulsion grew,
  I ran a dead-heat all the way.
I lost by yards at ten to 2.
  This is the seventh time today.

Prince, did the brandy fail you, too?
  You dreamt that arrowroot would stay?
My opium fairly galloped through.
  This is the seventh time today.

1915

Names

People in the life of Rupert Brooke whose names appear in these pages

Abercrombie, Lascelles, poet and professor of poetry, Leeds, 1921: beneficiary under RB's will.

Asquith, Arthur ('Oc'), son of the Prime Minister, fellow-officer in RND, one of RB's burial party.

Asquith, Violet (later Bonham-Carter) PM's daughter, close friend and confidante of RB.

Brooke, Alfred, RB's brother, ex-President of Cambridge Union: killed in action, Western Front, 1915.

Brooke, Justin, (no relation of RB), son of owner, Brooke Bond Tea, actor Marlowe Society.

Brooke, Mary Ruth, RB's mother: became (at Rugby) one of the first women magistrates, 1920.

Brooke, William Parker, RB's father: housemaster of School Field House, Rugby School.

Browne, Denis, schoolfellow and fellow-undergraduate, musician: a member of RB's burial party [see Shaw-Stewart, Asquith], killed in action, Gallipoli, 1915.

Browne, Maurice, impresario at Chicago and later in England, voyaged to UK with RB, 1914.

Cornford, Francis, teacher of classics at Trinity College, Cambridge, m. Frances Darwin.

Cornford, Frances (née Darwin), poet, granddaughter of Charles, member Cambridge Marlowe Society

Cox, Katharine ('Ka'), student at Newnham College, Treasurer Marlowe Society. Loved by RB

Dalton, Hugh, fellow undergraduate with RB, later Chancellor of the Exchequer under Attlee.

Darwin, Frances, granddaughter of Charles Darwin, m. Francis Cornford (see above).

De la Mare, Walter, poet, novelist and critic, beneficiary under RB's will.

Dent, Edward, Professor of Music, King's College, Cambridge. edited and published works of Denis Browne.

Eckersley, Arthur, resident Rugby town: dramatist, contributor to *Punch*.

Fry, Geoffrey (later 'Sir'), fellow undergraduate with RB at King's: became distinguished civil servant.

Gibson, Wilfrid ('Wibson' to RB), poet (Georgian and 'Dymock') friend of RB, beneficiary under his will.

Gill, Eric, artist and sculptor, lived in a community at Ditchling, carved *The Soldier* on RB's memorial plaque in Rugby School Chapel.

Hargreave, Ronald, painter, on voyage with RB on *S.S.Philadelphia*, 1914.

Housman, A.E., poet, Professor of Latin, Cambridge University, author of *A Shropshire Lad*.

Keynes, Geoffrey (later 'Sir'), surgeon, RB's school and university friend and bibliographer of RB.

Keeling, Frederick (Ben), undergraduate of Trinity College, Cambridge. Keen Socialist and Fabian.

Lucas, St. John, poet, critic, ed. *Oxford Book of French Verse,* scholar, resident in Rugby, RB's early mentor.

Marsh, Edward, civil servant, secretary to Churchill, patron of RB and other poets, ed. *Georgian Poetry*.

Masefield, John, poet, later Poet Laureate, friend and host to RB, advised him on his play *Lithuania*.

Monro, Harold, poet, editor: founder of the Poetry Bookshop: brother-in-law of M.Browne.

Moore G.E., Cambridge philosopher, author *Principia Ethica*, which influenced contemporary students.

Nesbitt, Cathleen, actress: beloved of RB.

Olivier, Noel, one of four daughters of a diplomat, RB's first love as a schoolgirl: became a doctor.

Russell-Smith, Hugh, RB's friend at school and university: killed in action 1917.

Raverat, Gwen, (née Darwin) a granddaughter of Charles Darwin: artist, wood-engraver and painter.

Raverat, Jacques, a French maths student at Cambridge: also artist, m. Gwen Darwin, d. of MS 1925.

Sayle, Charles, an under-librarian of the Cambridge University Library: kept open house for students.

Scholfield, A.F. ('Scho'), student at King's College: amateur drama producer; as librarian went to India.

Shaw, George Bernard, famous writer and dramatist: member of the Fabians.

Shaw-Stewart, Patrick, Oxford graduate: fellow officer in RND, i/c RB's burial party: killed in action 1917.

Spencer, Stanley, artist: lived and worked at Cookham-on-Thames, nicknamed 'Cookham' by RB

Strachey, James, at prep school with RB, graduate of Trinity, Cambridge: Freudian pyschoanalyst.

Strachey, Lytton, brother of James and also at Trinity: well-known writer, member Bloomsbury Group.

Taatamata, daughter of Tahitian tribal chieftain: loved by RB and the subject of the poem *Mamua*.

Van Volkenberg, Ellen, actress, wife of Maurice Browne: in ship with RB: played Daughter in *Lithuania*.

Webb, Sydney (later Lord Passfield) and Beatrice, husband and wife, pre-eminent Fabians: ran Fabian summer school.

Ward, Dudley, fellow undergraduate, great friend of RB: became an economist: RB's mother bought and gave him The Old Vicarage, Grantchester, after RB's death.

BIBLIOGRAPHY

Names in bold type are the shortened version by which works are referred to throughout the book.

Bonham-Carter   Violet Bonham-Carter, *Winston Churchill as I knew him*   (London: Eyre & Spottiswode and Collins, 1965)

Brooke, Democracy Rupert Brooke, *Democracy and the Arts*   (London: Rupert Hart-Davis, 1946)

Brooke, Phoenix   *The Phoenix*, Vols. 1 & 3 (Rugby School, 1904-5)

Brooke, Webster   Rupert Brooke, *John Webster and the Elizabethan Drama* (London: Sidgwick & Jackson, 1916)

Browne   Maurice Browne, *Recollections of Rupert Brooke*   (Chicago: Alexander Greene, 1927)

Delany   Paul Delany, *The Neo-Pagans: Friendship and Love in the Rupert Brooke Circle* (London: Macmillan, 1987)

Harris   *Song of Love: the Letters of Rupert Brooke and Noel Olivier*, ed. Pippa Harris (London: Bloomsbury, 1991)

Hassall   Christopher Hassall, *Rupert Brooke: a Biography*   (London: Faber & Faber, 1964)

Keynes, Gates   Keynes, Geoffrey, *The Gates of Memory* (Oxford: Clarendon Press, 1981)

Keynes, Letters   *The Letters of Rupert Brooke*, ed. Geoffrey Keynes (London: Faber & Faber, 1968)

Keynes, Poems   *The Poetical Works*, ed. Geoffrey Keynes   (London: Faber & Faber, 1946)

Keynes, Bibliography   Geoffrey Keynes. *Bibliography of the Works of Rupert Brooke* (Second edition. revised, London: Rupert Hart-Davis, London, 1959)

Lehmann   John Lehmann, *Rupert Brooke: his Life and Legend* (London: George Weidenfeld and Nicolson, 1980)

Marsh   Edward Marsh, *Rupert Brooke: A Memoir* (separate edn. revised, London: Sidgwick & Jackson, 1918)

Nesbitt   Cathleen Nesbitt, *A Little Love and Good Company* (London: Faber & Faber, 1975)

Pearsall   Robert Pearsall, *Rupert Brooke: the Man and Poet* (Amsterdam: Rodopi N.V., 1974)

Rogers *The Poems of Rupert Brooke: a Centenary Edition*, ed. & intro. by Timothy Rogers (London: Black Swan, 1987)

Index

Other books by Peter Miller:

The Rugby Centenary Brooke
The Cross of Skyros